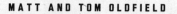

MATT AND TOM OLDFIELD

CLASSIC
FOOTBALL HEROES

MARADONA

FROM THE PLAYGROUND
TO THE PITCH

D0182848

DINO

First published by Dino Books in 2018,
an imprint of Bonnier Books UK,
The Plaza,
535 Kings Road,
London SW10 0SZ

🐦 @dinobooks
🐦 @footieheroesbks
www.heroesfootball.com
www.bonnierbooks.co.uk

Design and typesetting by www.envydesign.co.uk

Paperback ISBN: 978 1 78606 924 5
E-book ISBN: 978 1 78606 943 6

British Library Cataloguing-in-Publication Data:
A catalogue record for this book is available from the British Library.

Printed and bound in Great Britain by Clays Ltd, Elcograf S.p.A.

5 7 9 10 8 6 4

MIX
Paper from
responsible sources
FSC® C018072

For Noah and Nico,
Southampton's future strikeforce

CLASSIC
FOOTBALL HEROES

Matt Oldfield is an accomplished writer and the editor-in-chief of football review site *Of Pitch & Page*. Tom Oldfield is a freelance sports writer and the author of biographies on Cristiano Ronaldo, Arsène Wenger and Rafael Nadal.

Cover illustration by Dan Leydon.
To learn more about Dan visit danleydon.com
To purchase his artwork visit etsy.com/shop/footynews
Or just follow him on Twitter @danleydon

TABLE OF CONTENTS

CHAPTER 1

ARGENTINA'S WORLD CUP HERO

Mexico – 29 June 1986

Diego fixed the captain's armband on his sleeve and focused on glory. This had been his dream for as long as he could remember – to win the World Cup Final for his country, Argentina. In football, it didn't get any bigger or better than that.

'How are you feeling?' the manager Carlos Bilardo asked him in the dressing room. He was relying on his superstar, today more than ever.

'Ready,' Diego replied with a confident smile.

No-one had ever doubted the talent in the Argentina team. After all, they had Diego wearing the Number 10 shirt, the best and most expensive player in the world. Instead, it was the winning attitude that seemed to be missing.

Could they really go all the way and win it, just like they had at home in Argentina in 1978?

Or, with the pressure on, would they fall apart, just like they had in Spain in 1982?

That was the big question when the 1986 tournament began, and boy were Argentina answering it! South Korea, Bulgaria, Uruguay, England and Belgium – they had beaten them all. Under Diego's leadership, Argentina had been transformed from a squad of fighting misfits into a team with togetherness, strength and spirit.

Diego was in the best form of his life, but he couldn't win the World Cup on his own. Oscar Ruggeri and José Luis Cuciuffo in defence, Héctor Enrique and Jorge Burruchaga in midfield, Jorge Valdano in attack – they were all playing an important part in Argentina's success.

'Six down, one to go!' Diego kept reminding them of their tally of victories as the final drew near. 'Come on, guys, we're so nearly there!'

The last team in their way was West Germany. Diego wasn't at all surprised to be facing them in the final; when it came to big tournaments, they always found a way to win.

'Not today, though,' he told his teammates before kick-off. 'This is our day, our World Cup!'

In the tunnel, the Argentina players shouted and beat their chests like a band of gorillas. Other teams had been frightened by this, but not West Germany. Their players weren't scared of anything. Diego and co would have to beat them with their footballing skill instead.

As the two teams walked out onto the pitch in Mexico City, the 115,000 fans roared and waved their respective team's national flags: black, red and yellow for West Germany, and light blue and white for Argentina. Diego looked up at the rows and rows of blurred faces above. There were so many people waiting, hoping, expecting. He couldn't let his nation down, and he wouldn't. It was his duty to bring the World Cup home.

'Let's do this!' Diego clapped and cheered, looking along the line at his teammates.

When the game started, it soon became clear that West Germany's Lothar Matthäus was man-marking Diego, Argentina's danger man. Italy's Claudio Gentile had successfully stopped him back in 1982, but Diego was now older and wiser. Could he get the better of Matthäus when it mattered most? It wouldn't be easy. The German wasn't just a tough defender; he was also skilful and smart.

'You're not going anywhere,' Matthäus told him with an evil grin.

'We'll see about that!' Diego replied. He was desperate to grab another goal. What a tournament he was having. He'd scored two against England in the quarter-final – the 'Hand of God' and the 'Goal of the Century' – and then two against Belgium in the semi-final. A goal in the final would be the icing on the cake. It would prove once and for all that 1986 had been Diego's World Cup.

More importantly, however, he was desperate to win the final. When José Luis Brown and Jorge Valdano put Argentina 2–0 up, Diego was just as excited as everyone else. He didn't need to be the national hero every time.

'Keep going!' Diego urged his teammates. 'Remember, West Germany *never* give up.'

He was right. First, Karl-Heinz Rummenigge tapped one in. 2–1! Then, Rudi Völler headed home. 2–2!

'Uh-oh,' Diego thought to himself. For the first time all tournament, he was scared. What if West Germany scored again and stole the World Cup away from them? Argentina needed to dig deep and find a winner from somewhere.

'Come on, they're tired!' Diego shouted. 'Let's finish them off before extra time!'

In the centre-circle, he had six West Germany players around him, but he didn't panic. Somehow, when he was on the ball, time seemed to stand still. In a flash, he spotted a gap and he spotted Jorge Burruchaga's run. Diego hit the pass first-time and 'Burru' sprinted into the penalty area and scored. 3–2 to Argentina!

'Yes, you did it!' Diego screamed with delight.

'No, *we* did it!' Burru corrected his incredible captain.

Argentina still had six minutes to hold on. Bilardo

barked out frantic instructions on the touchline. 'No messing around! Mark up!'

Diego only knew one way to defend – attack. He linked up with the two Jorges one last time and stormed through the German defence. In the box, the keeper brought him down.

'Penalty!' Diego cried out, but the referee gave an earlier free kick instead. Argentina didn't mind – they were now seconds away from glory.

As West Germany launched one final ball upfield, Diego kept looking over at the referee, waiting for that whistle.

'Hurry up!' he muttered impatiently.

Finally, the referee raised his arms and blew. In that moment, Diego went crazy. He ran around, hugging everybody. 'We did it! We did it!' he shouted over and over again.

The Argentina fans invaded the pitch and soon Diego was at the centre of a big, chanting crowd.

Mar-a-Don-a! Mar-a-Don-a!

Vamos Vamos Argentina!

As he watched and listened to his nation's joy,

Diego burst into tears. Winning the World Cup was the greatest achievement of his life. He was so proud of his team.

'Come on, let's go get our trophy!' Diego told them.

As he held the World Cup for the first time, his hands were shaking. He looked at it lovingly and then lifted it high. He kissed it passionately, and then lifted it high again. He didn't want to let go.

'Hey, don't be greedy!' Jorge Valdano teased. 'Share it around!'

The Argentina players had achieved their wildest dream. They were returning home as world champions.

Back down on the pitch, the crowd carried Diego on their shoulders for a lap of honour. There was no feeling like it – love, pride and joy all merged into one. He felt like a king, the King of Football and the King of Argentina.

Chitoro and Tota's son hadn't just become a star; Diego had become his country's greatest star. He would go down in history. From the dirt tracks of Villa Fiorito, Diego was now Argentina's World Cup hero.

CHAPTER 2

VILLA FIORITO

The day of 30 October 1960 was bright and sunny in Villa Fiorito. For most of the local people, it was a Sunday like any other, filled with church, food and family time.

For the Maradonas, however, it was about to become a very busy Sunday indeed. Diego 'Chitoro' and Doña Tota already had four daughters and now their first son was about to be born. It would be another mouth to feed but they couldn't wait to welcome the new member of their family.

'Chitoro!' Tota called out, as she sat resting in a chair in the shade. She didn't panic at all. 'It's time!'

Her husband rushed around their tiny home,

collecting a few things to take to the Policlínico
Evita Hospital in Lanús – clothes, blankets, toys. The
family didn't have much but Chitoro wanted to make
sure that his first son was as comfortable as possible.

'Right, let's go!' he said, carefully helping his wife
up out of her chair.

'Wait,' Tota said suddenly.

Chitoro thought that it might be a false alarm,
but in fact, something shiny had caught Tota's eye.
'What's that?' she asked, pointing.

Their eldest daughter, Ana Maria, brought the item
over to her. It was a brooch in the shape of a star,
with glass beads that glistened like diamonds.

Tota smiled. 'Could you pin it to my dress please,
my darling?' she asked. 'It's a good sign. Our son –
your brother – is going to be a star!'

Chitoro and Tota had every reason to hope for
bigger and better things. Their family was one of
the poorest families in Villa Fiorito, which was itself
one of the poorest parts of Buenos Aires, Argentina's
capital city.

Life was a constant struggle and sometimes, the

family couldn't afford to eat. They lived in a small house with one small bedroom for the adults and one small bedroom for the children. The third room was where they cooked, ate and did everything except sleep. Every time it rained, the roof leaked.

The Maradonas had no running water in the house. Every day, they took it in turns to go to the tap down the street. They filled up big, heavy jugs to carry back for cooking, washing and drinking.

'Our children will grow up big and strong!' Chitoro liked to joke.

They hadn't always lived there in Fiorito, however. Chitoro and Tota were originally from the Corrientes Province in the north-east of the country. One day, they decided to move nearer to Buenos Aires, looking for better job opportunities.

Back home, Chitoro had been a boatman but in Fiorito, he worked as a bricklayer and a factory worker. He worked all day every day, but none of his jobs paid well. Tota stayed at home to look after their children, so it was up to him to earn enough money to put food on the table. That wasn't easy at all, especially now that there were seven of them.

'And boys eat more,' Tota warned her husband when they returned home from the hospital. 'Diego's got a very healthy appetite already!'

They had named their first son 'Diego' after his dad, and 'Armando', meaning 'soldier'. If he was really going to grow up to become a star, he had a fierce battle to fight. Growing up in Villa Fiorito was dangerous and difficult. There were so few jobs available that many kids in the neighbourhood were tempted into a life of crime. Diego, however, would be different. He was special.

'I mean, just look how much hair he's got already!' Tota laughed.

Chitoro and Tota were determined, and shared a belief that their son would be the one to help the family to escape from poverty.

Tota hoped that their son would grow up to be a kind and healthy person with a good, respectable job.

'Perhaps Diego will be an accountant,' she dreamt.

Chitoro hoped that their son would have opportunities that he never had growing up.

'If he studies hard, perhaps one day Diego will go to college!' he dreamt.

In the end, Diego chose a very different path, but he made his parents very proud. He did indeed help his family to escape poverty, becoming a bigger star than they could have ever imagined.

CHAPTER 3

ALWAYS PRACTISING

It wasn't long before Diego chose to follow his dad's dream, rather than his mum's.

It all started on his third birthday, when his cousin Beto Zarate gave him his first football. It wasn't a cheap, plastic one; it was a real leather one.

'Smell it,' Beto told him. 'It's just like the balls that the professionals use!'

That gift changed everything. Like Tota and her shiny brooch, Diego couldn't take his eyes off it.

'Just look at that smile!' Beto laughed.

Diego couldn't keep his feet off that ball either. He didn't even need coaching. As soon as it rolled near him, he knew what to do with it. He didn't just swing his little leg at it; he rolled it from one foot to the other, keeping the ball under control.

'Look at that skill!' Chitoro cheered.

Diego took his 'new friend' everywhere with him. Every night, he slept with the ball in his bed. He hugged it tightly to his chest, like he was protecting it from harm. Even in his dreams, Diego was always practising.

*

'No, you can't go out now – it's too hot!' Tota told her son. 'Wait until the sun goes down first.'

But Diego didn't have time to wait. His friends would start their football match without him and he didn't want to miss a single second.

'Please, mamá!' he begged.

Diego's Plan A was his angel face. He looked up at his mum with wide, innocent eyes and a big frown. That was usually enough to make Tota change her mind.

If that didn't work, however, he turned to Plan B – crying. 'Please, mamá!' he blubbered.

'Fine, out you go!' Tota gave in. 'But stay in the shade, okay?'

'Okay!' Diego lied. Their football matches always took place under the blazing sun. They played and played until they were about to collapse from exhaustion and heatstroke.

'Half-time!' someone would shout, and they stopped to get a drink of water from one of the houses nearby. If they had enough money, they sometimes bought a single slice of pizza and shared it between them, one bite each.

After a short break, they carried on until it was too dark to see the ball, or their parents called them home for food.

'At least we always know where he is,' Chitoro argued. He was happy to see his son playing football, even if it meant torn clothes and ruined trainers. The main thing was that Diego was safe and staying out of trouble.

'I'm starving! Did I miss dinner?' Diego asked, out of breath. His favourite football was still glued to his left foot. He was always practising.

*

'Diego!' Tota called out into the street. 'Come here,

I've got a job for you!'

In a flash, her son was there in front of her, waiting.
At the weekends, Diego loved running errands for his
mum. He liked to please her but that wasn't the main
reason for his eagerness. Running errands meant going
out on adventures in Villa Fiorito.

As a five-year-old, that was very, very exciting.
Diego could spend hours exploring the dirt tracks of
the neighbourhood and as long as he completed his
task, Tota didn't mind.

'What is it today, mamá?' he asked.

'Take this money to Señor Bernardo at the market,
my love,' she said, ruffling his hair.

'No problem, mamá. See you later!'

Before he set out on his journeys, Diego just had
one very important bit of preparation to do. Did he
have something to kick and juggle? Without that,
he couldn't – and wouldn't - go anywhere. Life was
boring without a ball. There was no way that he was
going to risk taking Beto's prized gift with him, so
what else could he practise with?

Sometimes, he kicked a rolled-up ball of paper.

Sometimes, he kicked an old orange that was no good for eating. And sometimes, he kicked a stone that he found along the way. Whatever he kicked, Diego was always practising.

*

'Diego!' Tota called out. 'Come on, it's time for school!'

This time, her son didn't race over to her. He didn't appear at all.

'Diego, this isn't funny. We're going to be late… again!'

In the kitchen corner, he stayed as quiet and still as possible. This was one of the benefits of being so small. Even in their tiny home, Diego could still find places to hide.

'Wait until I find you. You're in big trouble, young man!'

But eventually, Tota usually stopped looking for her son. She had lots of other things to do and besides, she had already given up on her dream of Diego going to college and becoming an accountant. Football was all he cared about, and football was where his talent lay. He could already do amazing things with a ball at his feet.

There were no qualifications needed to become a football star. It was all about natural skill, passion and practice. Diego ticked all three boxes.

'If this is our ticket out of poverty,' Tota told Chitoro, 'then we have to support him in every way.'

As soon as the coast was clear, Diego slipped out of his hiding place and rushed outside to play. He had a whole day of football ahead of him!

If there were other kids around, he challenged them to matches or skills competitions.

'I bet you an ice cream that I can beat you!'

If Diego was alone, that didn't stop him. Nothing could stop him. He still dribbled his ball around the dirt tracks and perfected his tricks. And if he ever got tired, he just kicked his ball against the battered wired fence, over and over again.

Left foot, then right foot, then left foot, then right foot...

Diego was always practising.

CHAPTER 4

ESTRELLA ROJA

After so much practising, it was soon time for Diego to test himself in proper football matches. Luckily for him, Chitoro had already started a youth team for the neighbourhood boys called *Estrella Roja* – 'Red Star'.

'We need you,' his dad told him, 'so far, we've lost every match!'

Around the corner from their house were seven little pitches, each belonging to a different local football team. One of these pitches was the home of Red Star. Diego couldn't wait to get started.

It wasn't much to look at. Their paddock – their *potrero* – was a hard, dirt pitch on a slope with bent, collapsing goalposts at either end. Every time someone kicked the ball, a cloud of earth flew up into the air.

'Pah!' Diego said, spitting out a mouthful of dust.

It wasn't exactly a football paradise, but he loved it from the second he stepped onto the *potrero*. Life felt so much better when he was chasing after a football and scoring goals. There was so much fun to be had.

In a matter of minutes, it became Diego's own *potrero*. He was still very small for his age, but he was far from skinny. He made up for his lack of height with plenty of power and determination, as opponents soon found out.

'Wow, who is this kid?' they asked, shocked, as Diego brushed aside their heavy tackles and kept dribbling towards goal.

At first, Chitoro put his son in defence, but it soon became clear that all Diego wanted to do was attack. Luckily, he was very good at it, head and shoulders above the rest. Dancing along the dirt tracks of Villa Fiorito had prepared Diego perfectly for this.

Instead of weaving past shoppers and market stalls,

he now weaved past defenders and goalkeepers.

Instead of controlling his rolled-up ball of paper across the bumpy bridge, he now controlled a real ball across a bumpy pitch.

No-one could get it off him. Diego switched from one foot to the other, never losing his balance, even in tight spaces. At times, it really looked a lot like magic.

'How on earth did he escape with the ball there?' Chitoro asked himself.

Diego burst forward, nutmegged one defender and then raced past another. As a third defender lunged towards him, he slipped the ball across to his teammate. *Goal!*

Diego wanted a goal of his own. He dropped deep to get the ball and then turned and *zoom*! He was off, past one tackle, then another, then another, then another. In the penalty area, he chipped the ball cheekily over the keeper. *Goal!*

Red Star's opponents sank to the dirt, exhausted and defeated. Eventually, Chitoro had to call his son over to the touchline.

'Okay, I think that's enough showing off for one day. Go easy on them for a bit. At this rate, those defenders will never want to play football again!'

'Sorry, papá,' Diego replied. 'I was just having so much fun!'

Chitoro smiled. He could still remember the glory of his own childhood football days. What a feeling it was to dance across the dirt, leaving defenders for dead.

'And *Diegito* is a million times better than I ever was at that age!' he thought to himself, excitedly. His son was a star in the making.

Red Star's big local rivals were *Tres Banderas* – 'Three Flags'. They owned another of the seven little pitches in Fiorito. Usually, Three Flags won every time but with Diego now in the Red Star team, anything seemed possible.

Diego was good friends with Gregorio 'Goyo' Carrizo, the son of the Three Flags manager. At school, they were teammates but on the *potrero*, they were opponents and enemies.

'May the best team win,' Goyo said to Diego as

they shook hands before kick-off.

'Come on, boys!' Chitoro shouted from the touchline. 'This derby is bigger than Boca Juniors vs River Plate!'

Red Star vs Three Flags quickly became Diego vs Goyo. Who would lead their team to victory?

Goyo dribbled the ball up the pitch and played a one-two with his teammate. He was one-on-one with the Red Star keeper. *Goal!*

Diego responded immediately. He sprinted through the whole Three Flags team as if they were just cones on the training field. *Goal!*

The score stayed neck and neck – 3–3, 4–3, 4–4, 4–5, 5–5…

Diego knew that he couldn't win the Fiorito Derby on his own. As the match went on, more and more players were marking him closely. That meant that his teammates were standing in space. He needed to get the ball to them quickly, before the final whistle blew.

Just when it looked like there was no escape, Diego produced another moment of genius. With

a back-heel flick, he nutmegged the Three Flags
defender and set up his Red Star teammate to score
the winner. 6–5!

'Yes!' Diego roared as he ran over to hug his
delirious dad. 'We did it!'

'Well played,' Goyo said, shaking his friend's hand.
'Man, I hate playing against you! Wouldn't it be
great if we could play on the same team? We'd be
absolutely unstoppable!'

CHAPTER 5

'LITTLE ONIONS'

Villa Fiorito was a small, tight-knit community. Word spread quickly, especially when it came to footballing talent.

'*Diegito* is an incredible player,' Goyo's father argued passionately. 'No offence, Chitoro, but I can't believe that he's not playing for a better team than Estrella Roja!'

Diego's dad nodded modestly.

'Trust me, he's way better than anyone that I play with for *Cebollitas*,' Goyo added. He was now playing for 'Little Onions', the youth team of top professional club, Argentinos Juniors.

Again, Diego's dad nodded modestly.

'If he's that good, has Francisco Cornejo seen him play?' their friend José Trotta asked.

'No, not yet, but I keep telling him about him,' Goyo replied.

Cornejo had been coaching the Little Onions for years. With Goyo now in the team, he wasn't looking for any more new signings. Besides, this 'Diegito' probably wasn't that good anyway. People were always recommending young players to him and most of them turned out to be awful. Why would this one be any different?

'Look, kid, I'm sorry,' Cornejo told him. 'Tell your friend to try one of the other local teams. We're full!'

But Goyo refused to give up, and eventually he got Cornejo to change his mind.

'Fine, bring him along next week,' the *Cebollitas* coach said, admitting defeat. 'But no promises, okay?'

When Diego heard the good news, he jumped for joy and hugged his friend. 'Thanks, Goyo, you're the best!'

After a bit of persuasion, Diego's parents allowed

him to go. This was it – his big chance to impress. If it went well, he could start climbing the ladder to the top of world football. If it went badly, however, his dream might be over. Most kids would have been nervous about a trial at a big team, but not Diego. He was ready and raring to go.

The journey to the Little Onions training ground took two hours on two different buses. Diego had never travelled so far from Fiorito before. Luckily, Goyo was there with him to show him the way.

'We're nearly there now, I promise,' he said when Diego started to tap the window impatiently. 'It'll all be worth it!'

But when they eventually arrived, the gates were locked.

'Sorry boys, there's no training here tonight,' Cornejo said. 'After all that rain, we need to protect the pitch for the next first team match.'

Diego's heart sank. What bad luck!

'We've come all the way from Fiorito,' he protested with tears in his eyes.

The *Cebollitas* coach couldn't just let them turn

around and go back home. He had an idea. 'Let's head down to Parque Saavedra and see what we can organise there.'

The boys formed two teams and this time, Diego and Goyo got to play together. 'Let's do this!' they said, bumping fists. The deadly duo ran riot, pulling off nutmegs and party tricks all over the pitch.

The first thing Cornejo noticed about Goyo's friend was his unusual shape and size. He was small but very stocky, with a big head and a puffed-out chest.

'That boy's only eight years old?' the coach thought to himself.

Cornejo had his doubts and those doubts doubled as soon as he saw Diego in action. The kid didn't play like an eight-year-old at all. He played with the confidence and class of an adult. The Little Onions couldn't get close to him. At one point, Diego dribbled forward, lifted the ball over the defender's head with a *sombrero* flick, and collected it on the other side.

'He's too good to be true!' Cornejo muttered.

In all his years of coaching, Cornejo had never

seen anyone with so much skill at that age. It was impossible! Perhaps it was a lie. At the end of the session, Cornejo asked to see Diego's ID card.

'Sorry, I don't have it with me,' he replied. 'I'm only eight, I promise!'

But the *Cebollitas* coach wanted to see proof. The next week, Diego returned and this time he had his ID card with him. Only then did Cornejo allow himself to get excited.

'Great, welcome to the team!' he said, shaking Diego's hand heartily.

Cornejo set about helping his new player to improve in every way possible. He bought Diego his first pair of boots and organised extra training sessions for him. The coach even took Diego to see a doctor about his growth issues.

'Please do what you can,' Cornejo asked. 'This boy is going to grow up to be a star.'

With Goyo wearing the Number 9 shirt and Diego wearing the Number 10 shirt, the Little Onions won an incredible 136 games in a row. Diego scored so many goals that he lost count. He was having the time of his life. The team travelled all over Argentina, beating any team that dared to take them on.

Nothing could stop Diego. He was determined to win. One day, he turned up for a game with seven stitches in his hand. Cornejo took one look and shook his head.

'Sorry Diego, but there's no way you can play like that,' he said.

'Please!' he begged. He didn't want to miss a second, let alone a match. 'My dad said it was fine.'

'It's true,' Goyo backed him up. 'I heard him!'

In the end, the manager gave in. 'Okay, you can play for the first few minutes, but that's it!'

The first few minutes turned into the full 90 minutes. Diego scored five goals and *Cebollitas* won 7–1.

When the Little Onions were finally defeated in a cup final, Diego sat down on the grass and cried and cried. He had forgotten what it was like to lose. It was the worst feeling in the world.

One of his opponents came over to comfort him. 'Don't worry, you're going to be the best in the world.'

That was Diego's aim and he was starting to take it very seriously. He wasn't playing Fiorito football anymore; this was the real thing. He watched more and more professional football, trying to learn from his heroes. He paid particular attention to the best left-footed attackers, like Norberto Alonso at River Plate and Rivellino from Brazil.

His favourite player, however, was the Independiente forward Ricardo 'El Bocha' Bochini. Diego loved to watch him in action, along with his strike partner, Daniel Bertoni. Together, they tore the defences in Argentina to shreds.

'Goyo, that's going to be us when we're older!' Diego declared excitedly.

Diego was the star of the show, and not just for the Little Onions. By the age of twelve, he was also part of the half-time entertainment at the Argentinos Juniors home games.

In the centre circle, he showed off his brilliant ball-juggling skills:

left foot, right foot, right knee, left knee, left shoulder, right shoulder, head

left foot, right foot, right knee, left knee, left shoulder, right shoulder, head

He made it all look so easy and natural. With the fans around *La Paternal* stadium cheering him on loudly, Diego allowed himself to dream big.

'I want to win the league with Argentinos,' he told an interviewer, 'and then the World Cup with Argentina.'

CHAPTER 6

ARGENTINOS JUNIORS

Diego raced through the Argentinos youth teams like they were defenders out on the pitch. After a few great games in the ninth division, he moved to the eighth, then the seventh, and before he knew it, he was on the verge of the senior team. Some players struggled with each step up, but not Diego. He rose to every challenge and proved himself at every level.

'That kid will go far!' said anyone lucky enough to see him play. 'He's a genius!'

Ten days before he turned sixteen, Diego received the best early birthday present ever. After training with the Argentinos Juniors first team, their manager Juan Carlos Montes took him to one side.

'Tomorrow, you'll be one of our substitutes against Talleres,' he told his young star. 'Be ready to come on!'

Diego was speechless. He ran all the way home to tell his parents the great news.

'Congratulations!' Tota cheered proudly.

'I just hope I get to play,' Diego said, trying not to get his hopes up. He wasn't the kind of person who could sit patiently on the bench.

'Of course, you will!' Chitoro assured him. He never stopped believing in his son's talent. 'And I'll be there at *La Paternal* to watch a star being born!'

'What about work? Tomorrow is a Wednesday and it's an afternoon game.'

'Don't you worry about that!' his dad replied. 'I'll just ask to leave a little early. I wouldn't miss this for the world!'

Soon, the whole of Fiorito knew about Diego's upcoming debut. He was the talk of the town.

'No pressure, then!' he laughed to himself.

During the first half, Diego sat on the bench, taking in the incredible atmosphere. He had experienced the roar of the crowd many times before during his ball-juggling shows, but being there as an Argentinos player felt even better.

Diego was buzzing so much that he couldn't sit still. His legs were shaking, his arms were twitching, and his heart was pounding. He already had the red club shirt on, with Number 16 on the back. Now, he just needed to get out there and play.

As half-time drew nearer, Argentinos were 1–0 down. Montes turned around and looked at him. Diego didn't look away. 'Are you ready, kid?' he asked with a smile.

Diego's pulse raced even faster. 'Of course!' he replied. Forty-five whole minutes of football? He had only expected ten, or fifteen at the most.

'Good, I want you to go out there and play like you always do,' Montes told him. 'Use all your tricks and nutmeg a few players if you can!'

After a quick warm-up, Diego jogged out onto the field. In that moment, he felt invincible. With a stadium full of Argentinos fans cheering him on, how could he fail?

Juan 'Coya' Cabrera was the defender with the tough task of marking him. He hoped to use his strength to stop the young attacker, but Diego was too clever for him. When he received the ball, he faked to go left and flicked the ball through Coya's legs. Nutmeg! The crowd loved him already.

Ooooolé!

Diego dribbled towards goal at top speed, his long, curly hair flopping from side to side. As he raced into the penalty area, he went for the wondergoal, but his shot flew high and wide.

The fans clapped and cheered. 'More, more!' they yelled.

'I'm going to need some help here!' the embarrassed Coya cried out to his teammates.

Diego was way too hot for just one defender to handle. The Talleres players had to gang up together to stop his silky skills. If they couldn't tackle him fairly, they tackled him unfairly instead.

'Arghhh!' Diego screamed as he fell down on the grass.

Fouls in the first team seemed to hurt a lot more.

He would need to get better at dodging and jumping if he wanted to avoid injuries. The experienced pros would be queueing up to teach Diego a lesson or two about life at the top level.

Argentinos still lost the match, but their fans didn't seem to mind. They were too busy talking about their new teen sensation.

'He made those Talleres defenders look like fools!'

'I can't wait to see more of that kid. He's incredible!'

'That left foot is a thing of beauty!'

For Diego, it was a day that he would never forget, the day that his amazing football career really started.

After that, he didn't look back. A month later, he scored his first Argentinos goal against San Lorenzo de Mar del Plata. Diego celebrated like he had won the World Cup.

'I'm living my dream!' he told his parents afterwards. It was an unbelievable feeling that was impossible to describe.

When he got his first Argentinos pay cheque, Diego knew exactly what he was going to do with it.

He had been waiting for this day since he was a little boy.

'Mamá, let's go!' he called out.

Tota looked confused. 'Where are we going?'

'You'll find out!' was all Diego would say.

In his first job, at the age of thirteen, Diego had cleaned old, abandoned houses, getting rid of all the dust and cockroaches. Every day on his way to work, he had passed a pizzeria called 'La Rumba' and the smells were amazing.

'When I have money, I'm going to bring Mamá here,' he promised himself.

It was his way of saying thanks for everything that Tota had done for him. All the torn clothes that she had mended, all the days when she had gone hungry to make sure that her son had food. The Maradonas had never been able to afford a meal at a restaurant but, thanks to Diego, their hard times were over.

'Order as much food and drink as you like,' he told his mum merrily as they sat down at the table. 'It's on me!'

A few hours later, almost all of Diego's pay cheque was gone!

Luckily, the money kept coming. In no time at all, Diego was Argentinos' Number 10 – and their captain too. He danced through defence after defence, using all the tricks that he had learnt in the *potrero* of Villa Fiorito. He twisted and turned, shifting his body one way and then the other, and all the time, the ball stayed glued to his magical left foot. There was just no way to get it off him.

Diego scored free kicks, penalties, wondergoals and tap-ins. He even scored a header or two, despite only being 5ft 5in!

Diego loved Argentinos, and Argentinos loved Diego. His teammates looked up to him, and the fans cheered his name every time he played.

Mar-a-Don-a! Mar-a-Don-a!

CHAPTER 7

ARGENTINA

News of Argentinos' wonderkid spread like wild fire, from *La Paternal*, through the streets of Buenos Aires, and then out through the other districts of Argentina. Only four months after making his club debut, Diego was included in the national team squad for a friendly match against Hungary.

'Congratulations!' Tota cheered proudly again, with tears in her eyes. When it came to her talented son, nothing surprised her anymore.

'I just hope I get to play,' Diego said. If he did, he would become Argentina's youngest ever player, aged 16 years, 3 months and 28 days.

'Of course, you will!' Chitoro assured him once

more. 'And we'll be there at *La Bombonera* to watch
an *international* star being born!'

Argentina's coach César Luis Menotti had picked
a young squad, but Diego was still the youngest
by a long way. Players like Leopoldo Luque, René
Houseman and Américo Gallego had been playing
international football for years.

'I was already playing for Atlanta when you were
born!' goalkeeper Hugo Gatti told him with a laugh.

Off the training pitch, Diego was a little shy and
awkward around the more experienced players. On
the training pitch, however, he showed them no
respect. When the juniors played a match against the
seniors, Diego stole the show.

With the ball at his feet, he came to life, weaving
his way past tackle after tackle. He played the
beautiful game with such energy and passion. Diego's
new Argentina teammates tried to stop him, but
he was too quick, too skilful and too strong. Even
fouling him didn't work. He just got back up and
carried on tormenting them.

'Wow, he's certainly got talent!' Menotti thought

to himself as he watched.

At the end of the session, the coach went over to speak to Diego.

'That was some performance, kid! If the match on Sunday is going well, you'll definitely get some game-time. Be ready!'

Diego was always ready. As he listened to Menotti's praise, he beamed with pride. On the night before the game, Diego stayed calm. On the morning of the game, Diego stayed calm. But as the team coach arrived outside the stadium, his legs began to tremble. There were so many people everywhere. Suddenly, it dawned on him that he was about to make his debut for Argentina. He was about to follow in the footsteps of greats like Alfredo Di Stéfano and Omar Sívori.

'This is a really big deal!' Diego realised.

On the bench, he sat and watched his team score goal after goal. Each time the ball hit the back of the net, Diego's heart beat a bit faster.

He remembered his manager's words – 'If the match on Sunday is going well, you'll definitely get some game-time.' His debut was getting closer and closer by the second.

Early in the second half, Argentina were 5–0 up. Menotti wouldn't get a better chance to introduce his young playmaker to international football.

'Maradona!' he called out.

Diego jumped to his feet in a flash and walked over to his manager.

'Stay calm and play like you always do,' Menotti told him. 'Use your skills and use your pace!'

Diego nodded eagerly and took a big gulp of air. This was it. As he warmed up along the touchline, the fans chanted his name.

Mar-a-Don-a! Mar-a-Don-a!

Diego couldn't believe it. How did they even know who he was? To stop his hands and legs from shaking, he tried to find his parents in the crowd, but it was impossible. Seven thousand people had watched his Argentinos debut at *La Paternal*. That had felt like millions but now, 70,000 people were watching his Argentina debut at *La Bombonera*.

'I've got to make a big impression here,' Diego

told himself. The 1978 World Cup was only a year away and he was desperate to play.

With thirty minutes to go, he came on to replace Leopoldo. Diego was officially now the youngest player ever to represent his country. It was a nice record to hold but it didn't mean anything. Playing at a World Cup – that meant everything. That was what football was all about.

It was Américo who gave him his first touch with a nice easy pass. Diego controlled the ball and threaded it through two Hungary defenders to find René.

'That's it, well played!' Américo encouraged him.

For Diego, it was a decent start to his international career, but he couldn't grab a sixth goal for Argentina. In fact, he wouldn't score for his country for two whole years.

That night, there was no chance of Diego sleeping. Instead, he turned on the TV and watched the highlights from the game, spotting all of his mistakes.

'No, Diego, wrong ball!' he screamed at the screen.

As the 1978 World Cup approached, Menotti had a big decision to make. There were twenty-five players at the training camp but only twenty-two could make the final squad. Who would be the three unlucky men to miss out? The fans wanted Diego to be included as a wildcard, but in the end, the coach chose more experienced players instead.

'I'm sorry, kid, but you're still a little too young,' Menotti told him. 'You'll play in other World Cups.'

Diego was devastated. It felt like his dream was over. He didn't want to play in other World Cups; he wanted to play in *this* World Cup, at home in Argentina. Age was just a number. He was good enough to play.

'If it was up to me, you'd be in,' Américo told him. 'I know you're hurting right now but Menotti is right. You *will* play in other World Cups.'

To make matters worse for Diego, Argentina went on to win the tournament without him, beating the Netherlands in the final.

'That could have been me!' Diego moaned as he watched a triumphant Mario Kempes lift the trophy. 'That *should* have been me!'

All he could do was use his anger to spur him on.

In his next game for Argentinos, Diego scored two and set up two. That kind of form would take him to the 1982 World Cup, no problem. By then, he would be twenty-one, with lots and lots of international experience. The national team would have no choice but to pick him.

Diego's first goal soon arrived, in June 1979, against Scotland. Leopoldo scored the first two, but Argentina's new Number 10 was determined to get on the scoresheet too. It would be the perfect way to complete his magical masterclass.

With twenty minutes to go, Diego had a one-on-one with the goalkeeper on the right side of the penalty area. He cut inside on his left foot and faked to cross the ball to the back post. As the keeper moved across, Diego shot for the near post instead.

Goooooooooooooooooooooaaaaaaaaaaaaaaaaalllllllllllll llllllllllllll!!!!!!!!!!!!!!!!!

Finally, Diego was off the mark! He threw his arms up in the air and jumped into Leopoldo's arms.

'There's no stopping me now!' Diego screamed with joy.

CHAPTER 8

WORLD CUP JUNIORS

Although Diego was already a star for Argentina's senior squad, he was still young enough to play for the Under-20s too. Menotti coached both teams and he was desperate for Diego to be his leader at the 1979 FIFA World Youth Championship in Japan.

'This is going to be your tournament,' his manager told him excitedly, 'and the whole world will be watching!'

Diego couldn't wait. It was the perfect way to put the disappointment of 1978 behind him and look ahead to 1982. Argentina had a very strong core, with Juan Simón in defence, Gabriel Calderón in midfield and, best of all, Ramón Díaz and their masterful Number 10 Diego in attack.

'If the seniors can win the World Cup, then so can we!' Diego told his teammates.

Argentina started with three wins out of three, against Indonesia, Yugoslavia and Poland. Ramón scored three goals, and Diego and Gabriel each scored two. The team was having so much fun together, attacking with style and skill. That was Diego's favourite way to play. They were entertaining everyone, especially the local Japanese fans.

'Right, the tough games start now!' Menotti told the players ahead of their quarter-final against Algeria.

But Argentina's young stars made it look so easy. Diego got the first goal, then Gabriel, and then Ramón grabbed a hat-trick. Diego cried when he was taken off. He didn't want to miss a minute.

'Okay, the tough games definitely start now!' their manager told them.

In the semi-final, they were up against their big South American rivals, Uruguay. Menotti was right. At half-time, the score was still 0–0, but team captain Diego didn't panic.

'We'll beat these guys,' he announced confidently in the dressing room. 'We just need to take our chances!'

Early in the second half, a chance fell to Ramón and he took it brilliantly. 1–0! Diego chased after his strike partner and gave him a big hug. 'We're nearly there!' he screamed.

Twenty minutes later, Argentina raced forward on the counter-attack. Ramón crossed to the back post and little Diego jumped up, unmarked, to head the ball home.

Goooooooooooooooooooooaaaaaaaaaaaaaaaaaallllllllllll llllllllllllllll!!!!!!!!!!!!!!!!!!!!

2–0! Diego ran towards the fans and slid across the grass on his knees. All of his delighted teammates chased after him and piled on top.

'We're in the final!' Gabriel cheered.

Fifty-two thousand supporters filled the National Stadium in Tokyo for Argentina vs the Soviet Union. With one more victory, Diego and co would be crowned Under-20 World Champions.

'Come on, so we're so close to lifting that cup!'

Menotti told his players.

In his head, Diego imagined returning home in glory. He imagined leading his team down the plane steps with the trophy in his hands, as the crowd clapped and cheered. What a proud moment that would be.

But, soon after half-time, and for the first time in the whole tournament, Argentina were 1–0 down. As Igor Ponomarev's header flew past their goalkeeper Sergio Garcia, Diego stood with the hands on his hips and kicked the air in frustration.

'Not good enough!' he muttered to himself. They couldn't let their country down like that, especially not in the final. They were the best team in the tournament by miles.

That goal, though, soon woke Argentina up. Their players raced around the pitch, intercepting passes and flying into tackles. Up front, Ramón and Diego were getting closer and closer to an equaliser, when suddenly, Gabriel's cross struck a Soviet Union defender on the arm. Penalty!

'Yes!' Diego cheered, punching the air.

Hugo Alves stepped up… and scored. 1–1 and advantage Argentina!

Diego passed to Ramón and kept on running. 'One-two!' he called out, but his strike partner had other ideas. Ramón dribbled all the way into the penalty area and shot past the keeper. 2–1!

The Argentina fans were up on their feet, waving their light blue scarves.

'What a goal!' Diego shouted as he joined in the big team celebrations. He considered that Gabriel had created the first goal, and that Ramón had scored the second – but what about him? Now, it was his turn to shine.

Diego got the ball in his own half and off he went, past one defender, and then another. As he entered the penalty area, he was knocked off balance and his cross got cleared away.

'Next time!' Diego told himself.

A few minutes later, he was fouled on the edge of the box. Free kick! Diego picked himself up and marched over to grab the ball. He had let Hugo take the penalty but there was no way that anyone else was taking this free kick.

Diego placed the ball down and took several steps back. There were six players in the Soviet Union wall, but he curled his shot round them and into the bottom corner.

Gooooooooooooooooooooaaaaaaaaaaaaaaaaallllllllllll llllllllllllllll!!!!!!!!!!!!!!!!!!!!!

Once he'd watched the ball hit the back of the net, Diego raced over to the corner flag and threw his arms up in the air.

'What a beauty!' Ramón cried out.

At the final whistle, Diego walked around the pitch, hugging each and every one of his teammates. 'We did it!' he kept saying. Argentina were the Under-20 World Champions. After one last tearful hug with Ramón, Diego walked up to collect the shiny silver cup.

'Everyone, make sure you've got a hand on it!' he called out behind him. '3... 2... 1...'

Campiones, Campiones, Olé! Olé! Olé!

As Argentina's captain, Diego was the one who lifted the trophy, but it was one big team effort.

They had achieved their dream together. Diego then passed the trophy to Menotti and they carried their manager on a lap of honour around the pitch.

Argentina! Argentina!

The party moved from the field to the dressing room and then back to the hotel. Diego did a lot more dancing than sleeping that night.

Ramón was the tournament's top goalscorer, but it was Diego who won the Best Player award. He had led Argentina to glory with his goals but also his creativity and character. After tasting glory in 1979 with the juniors, Diego was even more determined to do it again with the seniors in 1982.

CHAPTER 9

BOCA JUNIORS

With each and every game, goal and nutmeg, Diego's value rose higher and higher. He was one of the top scorers in Argentina, as well as the best playmaker. After five amazing seasons at Argentinos Juniors, however, he decided that it was time for a bigger challenge.

'I want to win trophies,' Diego told his mum Tota. 'I love this club, but we'll never be able to compete with the big boys like River Plate and Boca Juniors.'

Argentina's two top clubs were desperate to sign him. River Plate offered to make him their best-paid player. They already had a team full of stars including Américo and Daniel Passarella. Diego, however, had his heart set on Boca. It was the club that his family supported.

'I had the most amazing dream last night,' his dad Chitoro told him one day. 'You were playing for Boca at the Bombonera and I was there cheering you on!'

After that, Diego's mind was made up. 'Let's do this!' he decided.

Diego felt nervous ahead of his first day at Boca, but there was no need to be. He already knew Hugo Alves and Pichi Escudero from the Argentina Under-20s and his other teammates welcomed him warmly, especially after watching his first performances in training. He ran rings around the lot of them. Boca's defenders in particular were delighted to have him as a teammate, rather than an opponent.

'That kid is going to turn our fortunes around,' Roberto Mouzo predicted. 'He'll take us to the title!'

As part of the transfer deal, Boca played Argentinos in a friendly match. In the first half, Diego made one final appearance in the white and red of Argentinos.

'Here you go,' he said, handing his shirt to his old youth coach Francisco Cornejo at half-time. 'Thank you for everything!'

In the second half, Diego made his first appearance in the blue and gold of Boca. It was the start of an exciting new adventure.

Just two days later, he made his Boca debut for real. At the age of just twenty, Diego led the team out onto the pitch as captain. *La Bombonera* was bursting with noise and excitement. It was a very special occasion for the fans and they filled the air with confetti.

Diego! Diego! Diego!

It was the stadium where Diego had made his Argentina debut four years earlier. It felt really good to be back. So much had changed since then. Now, he was wearing the blue and gold Boca shirt, with Number 10 on the back. It was time to make his mark.

Diego scored twice and set up one for his new strike partner, Miguel Brindisi. Together, the club's new star strikeforce took the Argentinian League by storm with goal after goal, and Boca sat top of the table for the first time in years.

'Now, we've just got to make sure that we stay here!' the manager Silvio Marzolini told his players.

It was time for Boca's biggest game of the season, the *Superclásico* against River Plate. On a soaking wet night at *La Bombonera*, Diego was determined to lead his team to victory against their greatest rivals.

'I came here to win trophies,' he said in his pre-game team-talk, 'and that's what we're going to do. Come on!'

Diego had his dad there watching in the crowd. Chitoro had only ever seen one *Superclásico* before and on that occasion, Boca had lost badly. This time would be different.

As soon as the match kicked off, Diego was surrounded by River defenders. They tried to win the ball cleanly at first but when they couldn't, they played dirty. They kicked him and pushed him.

'Ref!' Marzolini cried out on the touchline. 'That's got to be a foul!'

Diego, however, never complained. He was used to the rough treatment and he just got back up and called for the ball again. What else could he do? If he got frustrated, he wouldn't be able to win the game for Boca.

No defence could stop him forever. Eventually, he always managed to escape. He dribbled all the way from his own half, dancing past flying, clumsy tackles. As he approached the River penalty area, he played a clever pass through to Hugo Perotti on the left. Perotti was fouled but the ball fell to Diego again. When the goalkeeper blocked his shot, Miguel was there for the rebound. 1–0!

'We're unstoppable!' Diego cheered, jumping up onto his strike partner's back.

Once Miguel scored the second goal, Diego went searching for the third. He didn't want to feel left out. As the cross came in from the right, he brought the ball down beautifully. With a drop of the shoulder and one quick tap of the left boot, he dribbled around the scrambling goalkeeper and then calmly shot past the defender on the line.

Goooooooooooaaaaaaaaaaalllllllllllllllllllllllll!!!!!!!!!!!

Diego made a wondergoal look so easy! He raced to the corner and slid across the mud on his knees.

'Is there anything you can't do?' Miguel joked as they hugged.

Diego shrugged and smiled. 'If there is, I haven't found it yet!'

In that moment, Diego was the happiest man in the world. He loved Boca – and Boca loved him. The players celebrated together with steak and chips.

'To the title!' Diego toasted.

'The title!' his teammates echoed.

Unfortunately, the league wasn't done and dusted yet. In the last weeks of the season, Boca won, lost, won, then lost. Ferro Carril Oeste were catching up.

As captain, it was Diego's job to turn things around. 'Come on, one final push!' he urged his teammates. 'We can't let this slip away!'

On the last day of the season, Boca just needed one more point to win the league title. In their final game, opponents Racing took the lead, but Diego calmly equalised with a penalty. It was only when the final whistle went, that he let his emotions out.

'Yes, yes, YES!' Diego shouted, running around like crazy. He was finally a champion at club level, and a champion with his beloved Boca.

CHAPTER 10

1982: A WORLD CUP TO FORGET

As the Argentina squad arrived in Spain for the 1982 World Cup, there were hundreds of journalists and football fans waiting for them. Argentina were the reigning champions with famous international stars like Daniel Passarella, Mario Kempes and Ossie Ardiles.

Most eyes, however, were on Argentina's youngest superstar. Diego had just signed for Spanish giants Barcelona for £5 million. That meant he was now the most expensive footballer on the planet, and 1982 was going to be his moment, his year, his World Cup.

'Diego! Diego!' voices called out. Cameras flashed

in his face and hands reached out for autographs.

'Welcome to Spain!' joked his national teammate
Jorge Valdano, who played for Real Zaragoza. 'You
better get used to all this attention.'

Diego smiled, 'Don't worry, I can handle the
pressure!'

It was a lot of pressure to handle, however,
especially at his first senior World Cup. There was no
time for Diego to soak up the amazing atmosphere.
Argentina's first match of the tournament was against
Belgium at the Nou Camp, the home of Barcelona.
The club's fans couldn't wait to see their new star
signing in action for his country.

Diego got the ball in midfield and brushed past the
first tackle.

Olé!

He played a neat one-two with his old Under-20
strike partner Ramón and then kept on dribbling
towards goal.

Olé!

In the end, a Belgium player hacked him down.
Sometimes, that was the only way to stop Diego. As

he rested on the grass to catch his breath, he clapped Ramón's pass. 'More of that!' he shouted.

But after that strong start, Argentina fell apart. They had spent four long, hard months preparing for the tournament, but suddenly the players looked tired and confused. Their spark was gone, even Diego's. In defence, they were all over the place, and eventually, Belgium took the lead.

'What's going on?' their manager Menotti screamed at them. 'Did you think this was going to be easy? You can't just walk your way into another World Cup Final!'

Diego did his best to rescue his country from a shock defeat. In the last few minutes, he sent a fierce, curling free-kick over the wall and towards the top corner. The Argentina and Barcelona fans got ready to celebrate a magical goal, but the ball struck the crossbar instead.

'Noooo!' Diego cried out, with his hands on his head. He had felt sure it was going in.

Never mind – he bounced back brilliantly in Argentina's next game against Hungary. His two

goals showed both sides of his footballing genius –
the strength and the skill.

For the first goal, he reacted quickly to a rebound.
He battled bravely to beat the defender to the ball
and score with a diving header.

For the second, he played a lovely one-two with
Mario and then fired a low, swerving shot past the
keeper.

*Gooooooooooooooooooooaaaaaaaaaaaaaaaaalllllllllllll
llllllllllllll!!!!!!!!!!!!!!!!!!!!*

Diego slid to his knees by the corner flag and roared
up at the cheering fans. It was an incredible feeling to
score for his country at a World Cup. After missing out
in 1978, he was making up for lost game-time.

With a win against El Salvador, Argentina made
it through to the second round, but their next two
matches would be against Italy and Brazil.

'Come on guys, we're ready for this!' their captain
Daniel shouted.

It was a tricky test for all of them but especially for
Diego. Italy had the toughest defenders in the world,
and Claudio Gentile was the toughest of them all. It

was his job to mark Argentina's star Number 10 out of the game.

'No problem!' Claudio told his manager, with an evil grin.

Everywhere that Diego went, Gentile followed right behind him like a dark shadow. Diego was a magician, a player who could escape from anything. But as hard as he tried, he couldn't escape from Gentile. The Italian defender was determined to stop him. He pushed him, pulled him, kicked him and tripped him.

'Referee!' Diego protested as he landed on the grass again.

Every time he got the ball, Gentile snapped at his ankles.

Every time he turned, Gentile blocked his path.

Diego didn't give up, though. He sent another fierce, curling free kick over the wall and towards the top corner. Italy's goalkeeper didn't even move but this time, the ball struck the post.

'Noooo!' Diego cried out once more, with his hands on his head.

It just wasn't his day, or Argentina's. They lost the game 2–1, which meant that they had to beat their South American rivals Brazil or be knocked out of the World Cup.

'We're too good to go home this early,' Menotti told his players before kick-off to fire them up. 'Think of all the people watching back home. Don't let them down!'

Diego was desperate to make his nation proud but how was he supposed to do that when defenders kept kicking him? Brazil played dirty, just like Italy.

Diego drifted all over the pitch, looking for the space to create something special. On the right wing, he escaped one crunching tackle and then another. As he entered the penalty area, the Brazil left-back chopped him down.

'Penalty!' Diego screamed.

The referee shook his head and waved play on.

'What? How is that not a foul?' Diego shouted angrily, stamping his feet.

After that, Diego grew more and more frustrated. It wasn't fair. Players had been fouling him all tournament and getting away with it. Enough was enough. Brazil were 3–0 up when Diego lashed out and kicked Batista. He knew what was coming. Red card!

Diego didn't complain. As he trudged slowly off the pitch, his teammate Alberto Tarantini patted him on the head. 'Unlucky, kid. They were out to get you today.'

It really wasn't the way that Diego wanted to leave his first World Cup. He had dreamt of so much better. Oh well, 1982 hadn't been his tournament, but he had plenty more ahead of him. With lessons to learn, Diego would come back bigger and stronger in 1986.

CHAPTER 11

BARCELONA BRILLIANCE

The Barcelona players watched Diego play for the first time at the 1982 World Cup. They noticed his lovely left foot, his dangerous dribbling and, of course, his hot temper. He looked like a very skilful new signing, but how would he cope with Spanish football? It turned out that they hadn't seen anything yet.

In his first training session at Barcelona, Diego got on the ball and didn't let go. He was the most expensive footballer in the world now, playing for the best club in the world. He needed to prove that he belonged there. He danced through the defence again and again. Even at top speed, the ball stayed stuck to his left boot.

His teammates stopped to watch and admire The Diego Show. It was a breathtaking sight.

'Wow, he's even better than I thought,' Barcelona's midfielder Bernd Schuster thought to himself.

'This guy's a genius!' winger Lobo Carrasco muttered to himself. He had never seen skill like it.

'If he can do that to us in practice,' centre-back Migueli wondered out loud, 'imagine what he can do to Real Madrid in a proper match.'

Barcelona vs Real Madrid was one of the greatest rivalries in world football. *El Clásico* was a famous fixture, even in Argentina. Whether the game was at the Nou Camp or the Bernabéu, the atmosphere was unbelievable. Nothing could beat the noise, the colour and the tension of a stadium filled with 90,000 passionate fans.

'Just you wait,' Lobo told him. 'You've never felt anything like it!'

Diego couldn't wait to get stuck in. By the time they played the first *El Clásico* of the season, Barca were only three points behind Real. A win away at the Bernabéu would level things up, and Diego knew that a match-winning performance would make him an instant fans' favourite.

'Come on, we can do this!' their captain, Quini, told them before the big kick-off.

After looking around the dressing room, his eyes stayed on Diego. These big games were made for big players like him. He had won the *Superclásico* for Boca, and now it was time to win *El Clásico* for Barcelona.

When his team needed him most, Diego came alive. He raced around, causing Real Madrid problems all over the pitch. It was his lovely left foot, however, that won the game for Barcelona.

Early in the first half, he threaded a brilliant pass through to Esteban Vigo, who rounded the goalkeeper and scored. 1–0!

'What a run!' Diego cheered, jumping into Esteban's arms.

'What a pass!' Esteban replied.

In the second half, Diego did it again. This time, he dribbled through two tackles before sliding the ball across to Quini, who lobbed the keeper. 2–0!

The Real Madrid fans sat in stunned silence, but their Barcelona rivals made more than enough noise to fill the stadium.

'What a finish!' Diego cheered, jumping into Quini's arms.

'What a pass!' he replied.

At his best, Diego was the biggest big game player around. When his team needed a moment of magic, or a touch of class, he got the job done. The fans loved their new hero.

Diego! Diego! Diego!

Nothing could stop Diego from playing in the second *El Clásico* of the season, not illness and not injury. He had been looking forward to the fixture for months. Could he be Barcelona's hero again? After two assists in the first game, he wanted a goal of his own this time. He was fired up and ready to go.

Real Madrid took the lead, but Diego popped up in the penalty area with a clever header just before half-time.

Gooooooooooooooooooooaaaaaaaaaaaaaaaalllllllllllll llllllllllllll!!!!!!!!!!!!!!!!!!!!

He ran towards the fans shaking his fists with joy. 'Come on, let's go and win this!' he cheered.

With time running out, Bernd chipped a great pass to Diego on the right side of the penalty area. His first-time cross flew just over Lobo's head but bounced down in front of Periko Alonso. 2–1 to Barcelona!

Diego's legs had started to feel tired, but suddenly he was full of energy again. He chased after Periko and piled on top of him.

'This is why I love football so much!' Diego thought to himself.

Even after tormenting Real Madrid twice, he still had another three *El Clásicos* to enjoy. He was determined to finish his first year in Spain with at least one trophy, if not two.

'They can't handle me!' he boasted confidently.

First up was the Spanish Cup Final in Zaragoza. Diego started in style. When he got the ball from Bernd, he weaved his way through three flying tackles and somehow stayed on his feet. The fourth Real Madrid challenge, however, knocked him to the floor.

Diego! Diego! Diego!

The Barcelona fans loved his amazing attacking runs. Diego didn't create a goal that time, but he kept on trying until he did. With thirty minutes gone, he chased after Bernd's brilliant long ball, cut inside past the first defender and set up Víctor Muñoz. 1–0!

'Get in!' Diego shouted, punching the air. As he looked up to the stands, he saw a raging sea of blue, red and yellow. Winning *El Clásico* meant so much to the people of Barcelona.

When Real Madrid equalised, it looked like the game was going to extra time. Diego's legs were battered and bruised from all the kicks, but he never gave up and neither did his teammates. In the ninetieth minute, Marcos Alonso scored an amazing diving header to win the cup for Barcelona.

'We did it!' Diego screamed out as he joined in the team celebrations. 'The Spanish Cup is ours!'

The League Cup, however, was still up for grabs. The Real Madrid players were hungry for revenge, but Diego was hungry for more glory. In the tense second half at the Bernabéu, Bernd passed forward to Lobo, who slid the ball across to Diego.

Diego was through on goal! It was a long way to dribble from the halfway line, but he could run faster with the ball than without it. In the penalty area, he tricked his way past the keeper and got ready to pass into the empty net...

But out of the corner of his eye, Diego spotted a Real Madrid defender sprinting over to him. He thought back to his childhood days playing on the *potreros* of Villa Fiorito. If there was the chance to dribble past one more player, you always took it.

'Why not?' Diego thought to himself. He didn't care that it was a cup final. He was a born trickster and a born entertainer. He waited for the defender to slide in for the tackle and then pulled the ball back brilliantly and tapped it in.

Goooooooooooooooooooooaaaaaaaaaaaaaaaaalllllllllllll llllllllllllll!!!!!!!!!!!!!!!!!!!

'Yessssss!' Diego roared up at the sky, with his arms up like a champion.

The stadium went wild, and it wasn't just the

Barcelona corner. The Real Madrid fans never clapped their rivals. It was unheard of, but after that audacious bit of skill, Diego deserved the applause.

'Wow, that Maradona is a special footballer!' they said to each other.

Even though Diego had stolen the Spanish and League Cups away from them, the Real Madrid supporters still appreciated footballing genius when they saw it.

CHAPTER 12

BARCELONA BLUES

Diego's time at Barcelona was no fairy tale, however. For every success, there was also a setback. Each time he felt like he was finding his best form, something went wrong.

'I'm cursed!' Diego decided eventually.

In his first season, it took him a while to get used to Spanish football. The game was played at a much faster pace than in Argentina and he struggled to keep up.

'Run!' Barcelona's German manager Udo Lattek shouted at him.

'I'm trying!' Diego barked back.

As a Number 10, that just wasn't his style. At

Argentinos and Boca, he would get the ball first and then start running. Diego's best asset was his skill *with* the ball. Running without it felt pointless, but Diego didn't complain. Instead, he worked hard to get fitter and stronger.

'That's it!' Lattek urged him on.

As the season went on, Diego adapted to Barcelona, and Barcelona adapted to Diego. But just when they started to look invincible, he fell seriously ill. The timing was terrible. The only answer was four months of rest, sixteen whole weeks without football. What a nightmare!

'What am I supposed to do now?' he asked, but the doctor didn't have the answer for that.

Diego suddenly felt very far from home. He missed Argentina, he missed his family, and he missed the love of his life, football. If he couldn't play it, he definitely didn't want to watch it on TV.

'Come out for a drink with us!' his Barcelona teammates suggested, but he said no and stayed at home instead.

Thankfully, Diego's mum Tota came over for

Christmas and helped to raise his spirits during that dark spell. She took one look at her sad son and told him to shape up.

'You're behaving like your career is over, but it's not. Don't be so dramatic! When bad things happen, we battle on, my love. Armando is your middle name. You're supposed to be a soldier – start acting like one!'

After that telling-off from his mum, Diego had no choice but to cheer up and come back stronger.

But it wasn't easy. In his first season, the problem had been illness, but in his second season, it would be injury.

'My body is homesick!' he joked, trying to stay positive.

The more goals Diego scored, the more kicks he received. The Spanish defenders would do anything to stop him and the referees did nothing to protect him. After his training in Argentina, Diego was able to dodge almost anything, but one terrible tackle left him hurting for months.

Barcelona were cruising to a 4–0 victory at the

Nou Camp and their opponents, Athletic Bilbao, were furious about that. One player in particular, Antoni Goikoetxea, charged around the pitch like a raging bull.

'Calm down!' his teammates tried to warn him, but he didn't listen.

Unfortunately, Diego was the player that Goikoetxea was marking. As the little Argentinian got the ball and turned to dribble, he felt the studs of a boot crash into his left leg. *Whack!* It sounded like a piece of wood snapping in half.

'Arghhhh!' Diego screamed in agony. He knew straight away that it was serious.

Migueli raced over to his teammate. 'What's wrong?' he asked.

Diego just kept shaking his head. He was in too much pain to speak. Eventually, he managed to cry out, 'I'm broken! I'm broken!'

Diego left the field on a stretcher, covering his face to hide the tears. What now? Was his season over?

'You're going to be fine,' the club doctor reassured him, 'but you will need an operation.'

An operation! Diego had never had an operation in his life. As he arrived at the hospital, he was terrified. What if it went wrong and he could never play football again?

'Stay strong, you're a star!' Menotti told him. His old Argentina manager was now his Barcelona manager too.

Once the operation was over and his leg started to heal, Diego's next thought was, 'Right, when can I play again?'

He went back to Buenos Aires and worked hard on his recovery. But every time he asked Menotti, he got the same frustrating answer: 'Not yet, be patient.'

Barcelona were trying to look after Diego. They didn't want to rush their superstar back too quickly and make his injury worse. Diego, however, didn't see it that way. He needed football. Without it, he didn't know what to do with himself.

When Diego returned to the pitch, he hoped it would make him happy again. Unfortunately, this time, it wasn't the answer. He was fed up with Spanish football – the constant running and the constant fouling. Diego just wanted to play the beautiful game his way. He wanted to entertain the fans and have fun with the ball at his feet. Was that really too much to ask?

Apparently so. In the 1984 Copa del Rey Final, Barcelona faced Athletic Bilbao again. Diego was up against his enemy Goikoetxea once more. Instead of revenge, however, he got more kicks and more abuse. When Barcelona lost 1–0, Diego lost his temper out on the pitch. He wasn't proud of his angry actions, but he'd had enough. He hadn't won La Liga, but two cups would have to do. His eventful spell in Spain was over.

'Who wants me?' Diego asked his agent. 'I'll go anywhere!'

CHAPTER 13

NAPOLI

Napoli had first tried to sign Diego back in 1979 when he was still playing for his first club, Argentinos Juniors. One day, five years later, he returned to his hotel room to find a parcel from Italy. Inside, was a light blue football shirt with the Number 10 on the back, and a letter:

Dear Mr Maradona,
We'd like to invite you to come to Naples and
visit our beautiful city and our fantastic football
club. We have no doubt that you'll love it here.
At the moment, we are unable to buy foreign
players but as soon as that rule changes, we
want to make you our first big signing.

Diego didn't know much about Napoli, but he never forgot that letter. Five years later, as he looked for another new club, there was lots of interest from Italy. Who wanted Diego the most?

Juventus? No – their president Giampero Boniperti shook his head. 'He's too small to make it big in Serie A.'

AC Milan? Inter Milan? No, in the end, it was Napoli who wanted him the most. They agreed to pay Barcelona £7million and make Diego the most expensive player in the world again.

'Right, let's do this!' Diego decided straight away.

When he arrived in Naples, he thought he would just sign the contract, pose for a few photos and then leave. He was expecting a quiet event but instead, there were 80,000 fans in the Stadio San Paolo to welcome him. It was even bigger than his Boca arrival.

'Wow, I love this club already!' he thought to himself.

As Diego walked out of the tunnel and onto the pitch, the Napoli fans roared.

As Diego lifted his arms up and waved, they roared louder still.

As Diego kicked a ball into the crowd, they roared *even louder.*

In the middle of the pitch, the club had rolled out a light blue carpet for him to stand on. With a Napoli scarf around his neck and a microphone in his hand, Diego spoke the only Italian that he knew.

'*Buona sera. Sono molto felice di essere con voi.*'

'Good evening. I am very happy to be here with you' – they weren't exactly exciting words, but the fans went wild anyway. They had even made up a song for Diego already:

'*Maradona, take charge...*
Your Argentina is here... '

When he left the pitch a few minutes later, Diego was in tears. What an amazing welcome! He was buzzing about his fresh new start at Napoli. He felt the same excitement that he had felt when he started out at Argentinos and then at Boca. He had found his new football home.

'I want to become a hero for the poor children

of Naples,' Diego told the local media, 'because growing up in Buenos Aires, I was just like them.'

It was a strong statement to make, especially before he had even kicked a ball for his new club, but Diego had his passion back. He was determined to live up to the fans' great expectations.

'I'm going to prove Boniperti wrong,' he told his new manager, Rino Marchesi. 'Football is about skill, not size!'

Before the season started, however, Diego had lots of work to do. The Italian defenders were the best in the world. The memories of Claudio Gentile at the 1982 World Cup still haunted him, and they also spurred him on. With the help of his own personal physio, Diego got fitter and stronger.

'Now, I'm ready!' he told his new teammates.

To prove it, Diego scored an incredible scissor-kick goal in training. As the ball flew into the top corner, jaws dropped everywhere. The coaches, the players, the spectators – none of them had ever seen anything like it.

'That guy is a genius!' the Napoli fans cheered.

With Diego in their team, they dared to dream that their club could win the Serie A title for the first time in history.

It was going to take time, however. By Christmas, the club was near the bottom of the table, not the top. They were fighting relegation. The Italian League was very competitive, with lots of top teams and lots of top talent. Juventus had Michel Platini and Paolo Rossi, Fiorentina had Sócrates and Daniel Passarella, and Inter Milan had Alessandro Altobelli and Karl-Heinz Rummenigge.

Napoli had Diego, but who else? At Barcelona, he had played alongside world-class players like Bernd and Lobo. At Napoli, he had his Argentinian teammate Daniel Bertoni, but most hopes rested on Diego's shoulders. It was his biggest test yet.

'Come on, we can do this!' he shouted in the dressing room. 'It's time to turn things around!'

At home to Lazio, Diego kept dribbling and driving Napoli forward. At half time, it was still 0–0, but he was feeling confident.

'Don't worry, the goals are coming!' he urged his teammates.

As a Lazio defender went to head the ball back to his goalkeeper, Diego pounced. He took one quick touch and then fired a shot past the keeper.

Goooooooooooooooooooooaaaaaaaaaaaaaaaaalllllllllllll llllllllllllllll!!!!!!!!!!!!!!!!!!!!!

The Stadio San Paolo erupted with noise. Diego to the rescue! He slid towards the corner flag on his knees to celebrate with the fans.

Twenty minutes later, Diego pounced again. This time, he stole the ball from a defender outside the penalty area. With the Lazio goalkeeper off his line, he went for an outrageous chip. If anyone could do it, Diego could! As he fell to the floor, he watched his shot sail over the keeper's head and into the top corner.

Goooooooooooooooooooooaaaaaaaaaaaaaaaaalllllllllllll llllllllllllllll!!!!!!!!!!!!!!!!!!!!!

The Napoli fans roared even louder and sang their hero's song at the top of their voices:

'Maradona, take charge...

Your Argentina is here...'

To complete his incredible hat-trick, Diego curled a corner-kick straight into the net. 'Yes, yes, YES!' he cheered, jumping up and down just like the fans in the stands.

Thanks to Diego's masterclasses, Napoli climbed the table and finished the 1984–85 season safely in eighth place. With some good new signings, they finished the next season in third place.

'Well done guys, we were only six points behind Juventus,' Diego said with a smile. 'That's nothing. Next season, we're going to win the Serie A title for sure!'

CHAPTER 14

1986: A WORLD CUP TO REMEMBER

But before that, Diego had a World Cup to win. He had been looking forward to the tournament ever since Argentina's disappointment in 1982. Diego was determined to make things right and make his country proud. The national team's new manager, Carlos Bilardo, had exactly the same plan.

One day in 1983, as Diego got ready to go running along the beach in Barcelona, Bilardo appeared at his front door.

'Sorry, I'm just heading out,' he explained.

'No problem, can I come with you?' his manager asked.

Diego was too shocked to say no. Why had he

come all the way to Spain? As they jogged along the coast, it all became clear.

'You're our most important player,' Bilardo told him, 'and the best player in the world. If you agree, I want you to be our new captain.'

Now, Diego was totally speechless. It had always been his dream to lead his country. It was a role that he was born to play. He had captained Argentinos, Boca and Napoli, and now he would captain Argentina. For years, he had been collecting armbands from all over the world, just in case that special day ever arrived. Now, he would be able to wear them all! As tears filled his eyes, he couldn't wait to tell Tota. She would be so, so proud of her son.

'Are you sure?' Diego asked. 'I'm still only twenty-four and Daniel–'

'I'm sure,' Bilardo confirmed. 'You'll be our new leader.'

'Thank you, I won't let you down! I'm going to make this Argentina team the best and most important thing in the world. We'll win that World Cup!'

Diego was ready to give every last scrap of energy for his beloved blue and white. During World Cup qualification, he travelled all the way from Italy to South America and then back for every match. It was a long and tiring journey, but it was all worth it to be the national team captain.

Argentina weren't playing well but, thanks to hard work and team spirit, they eventually made it through to the 1986 World Cup in Mexico.

'Give us time and we'll make you happy,' Diego promised the anxious Argentine people.

But in the build-up to the big tournament, everything went wrong. First, Argentina lost against France and Norway. Now, the nation really feared the worst.

'We're not even going to make it past the group stage!' some people predicted.

Then, the players started fighting amongst themselves. It was the old versus the young, the obedient versus the rebellious. The atmosphere in the camp was tense and toxic. As the captain now, Diego knew that it was his job to sort things out.

'Look guys, I know we have our differences, but now we must put them aside and work together,' he told his teammates passionately. 'The World Cup is only a few days away, so let's focus and win it for our country!'

If it was going to be Diego's tournament, he couldn't do it alone. The whole squad had to stay strong and united to prove their doubters wrong.

'We can take on anyone,' Bilardo told his team. 'We just need to believe!'

In their opening game of the tournament, it only took six minutes for Argentina to take the lead against South Korea. Diego's free kick hit the wall and bounced back to him. Instead of taking a wild swing at the ball, he nudged a clever header over to his strike partner, Jorge Valdano. 1–0!

The South Koreans tried to stop Diego with dirty kicks, trips and elbows, but nothing worked. He had learnt his lesson from 1982. Instead of responding with anger, Diego responded with his lovely left foot. Ten minutes later, Oscar Ruggeri made it 2–0 from another one of his fantastic free kicks.

What a start! Argentina's doubters were changing their minds already. 'Maybe they won't be so bad after all!' they said.

Just after half time, Diego completed his hat-trick of assists. He dribbled down the right wing, past one defender and then another. In the penalty area, he crossed to Jorge for a simple tap-in. He hadn't scored, but there was no question about Argentina's man of the match:

Mar-a-Don-a! Mar-a-Don-a!

First challenge: completed. Next up: Italy. There was no Claudio Gentile this time, but Gaetano Scirea and Pietro Vierchowod were just as tough and just as clever. Diego had faced them both while playing for Napoli.

'Be smart and be brave,' he told his teammates. 'Let's show them that we've come a long way since 1982!'

When Italy scored an early penalty, Argentina looked like they were in big trouble. Diego didn't see it that way, though. He was like an annoying little fly, buzzing all over the place. Again and again, he dribbled at the Italian defence, creating chances for his team to score.

'Believe!' Diego clapped and cheered. 'Believe!'

Argentina kept attacking. Ricardo Giusti passed to Jorge, who flicked the ball on into the penalty area. Scirea had a head start but Diego was far too fast for him. With his first touch, he steered the ball beautifully past the goalkeeper before he even knew what was happening.

Goooooooooooooooooooooaaaaaaaaaaaaaaaaalllllllllllll llllllllllllll!!!!!!!!!!!!!!!!!!!

Diego was delighted. It was one of his best ever goals and what a time to score it! He leapt over the advertising boards to celebrate right in front of the fans. Their blue and white national flags were waving for him.

'You genius!' Oscar Garré cheered, lifting Diego high into the air.

Diego's words had worked. The players had put their differences aside. Now Argentina were eating together as a team and playing together as a team. After a 2–0 win over Bulgaria, they made it through to the Round of 16.

'Three down, four to go!' Diego cheered happily.

With everyone behind him, he was playing some of the best football of his life. Even his mum was a little surprised at the extra spring in his step.

'What's got into you?' Tota asked on the phone. 'You're running faster than ever!'

Diego shrugged. 'You know me, mamá. I'm determined!'

Argentina hadn't beaten their South American rivals Uruguay at a World Cup since 1930. It was a fierce and bruising battle, but Diego's team didn't mind that. Pedro Pasculli got the single goal that Argentina needed and together the team held on until the final whistle.

'Four down, three to go!' Diego cheered happily.

CHAPTER 15

THE HAND OF GOD AND THE GOAL OF THE CENTURY

Diego's Argentina were through to the World Cup quarter-finals and yet still, no-one seemed to believe in them – except themselves, of course.

'We'll beat any team that gets in our way!' they cheered confidently.

Next up: England in the quarter-finals. After a slow start, Bobby Robson's boys had been getting better and better. Their star striker, Gary Lineker, was the tournament's top scorer.

'No mistakes today!' Bilardo reminded his players before kick-off. 'One mistake and we'll be heading home.'

Diego was desperate to make sure that didn't happen. In the hotel room he shared with Pedro, they had put up decorations to make it feel like home – fan letters, family photos, Argentina flags. They were expecting to be there for the full month, until after the World Cup final.

'Only once we become champions,' Diego told his teammates, 'can we return home.'

After a frustrating first half against England, Argentina came out fighting in the second. Diego dropped deep to get the ball and then drove forward. With a quick tap of his left boot, he dribbled past one player and then raced into the space between England's defence and midfield. As a Number 10, that was his favourite space.

When Diego ran out of room, he passed to Jorge, who tried to flick the ball back for the one-two, just like he had against Italy. Steve Hodge read it well, but he sliced his clearance back towards his own goal…

…where Diego had kept running into the box. As the ball dropped, he somehow outjumped the big England goalkeeper, Peter Shilton.

Goooooooooooooooooooaaaaaaaaaaaaaaaaallllllllllll llllllllllllllll!!!!!!!!!!!!!!!!!!!

As Diego ran off to celebrate, the England players raised their arms and shook their fingers. 'Ref, that was a handball!' they cried out.

They were right. It was Diego's hand, not his head, that had knocked the ball into the net. The referee and linesman, however, had been fooled and Argentina were 1–0 up.

'Shhhhhhhhhh!' Jorge said, putting a finger to his lips. 'Stop waving your hand in the air! They'll take your goal away.'

Four minutes later, Diego scored again. This time, he scored with his lovely left foot and soon, it would be known as 'The Goal of the Century'.

When he got the ball, the England fans booed, and the England players snapped at his ankles. Diego was now national enemy number one. Peter Reid and Peter Beardsley were the first to rush in, but with three touches and a neat turn, Diego escaped between them.

Olé!

As he raced down the right wing, he cut inside past Terry Butcher and then danced through Terry Fenwick's tackle.

Olé! Olé!

Diego was into the penalty area and, as Shilton rushed out in front of him, he tricked him with a dummy. He pretended he was going to pass across to Jorge but carried on dribbling instead.

Olé!

That was enough entertainment for one goal. As another England defender slid in to stop him, Diego tapped the ball into the empty net.

Gooooooooooooooooooooaaaaaaaaaaaaaaaaalllllllllllll llllllllllllllll!!!!!!!!!!!!!!!!!!!!

The stadium was a scene of total shock. Had that really just happened? Yes, the impossible had just happened. The England players sat slumped on the grass, and their fans sat slumped in their seats. Meanwhile, Diego led his teammates over to the Argentina fans and they all went wild together.

Mar-a-Don-a! Mar-a-Don-a!

No-one could believe what Diego had just done,

not even Diego himself. He had never scored a better goal, not even on the *potreros* of Villa Fiorito as a young boy. He had scored the goal of his life in a World Cup quarter-final. Nothing would ever compare to that moment of magic.

'I've never seen anything like it,' Oscar argued. 'That goal will go down in history!'

'Yes, but it was a bit selfish,' Jorge teased. 'I was there, waiting for the pass, and it never arrived. If you'd missed that, I would have killed you!'

After the game, the journalists asked Diego more questions about his first goal than his second.

'Was it a handball?'

'Did you mean to strike it with your arm?'

Diego sat there at the press conference and smiled. He was in a mischievous mood after beating England.

'It was a bit of the head of Maradona,' he announced, 'and a bit of the hand of God.'

In the semi-finals, Argentina faced Belgium. The players now felt like they were invincible, but Diego warned them not to get too confident.

'Just because we believe we're going to win

this, doesn't mean we're going to win it,' he told them. 'If we switch off, we'll lose. We have to keep playing like we've been playing all tournament.'

In the end, Diego scored both goals again but this time, it was a real team effort.

For the first, Héctor Enrique passed to Jorge Burruchaga, who drifted infield, looking for options. At the perfect moment, he played the perfect through-ball to Diego. All Argentina's captain had to do was lift it over the goalkeeper.

Goooooooooooooooooooooaaaaaaaaaaaaaaaalllllllllllll llllllllllllll!!!!!!!!!!!!!!!!!!!!

Diego ran straight over to hug his teammate. 'Burru, what a ball!'

For the second, it was José Luis Cuciuffo who dribbled forward and played a great pass to Diego. Once he had the ball, it was game over. In his form, who was going to stop him? Certainly not the tired Belgium defence. Diego raced through and smashed the ball into the net.

Goooooooooooooooooooooaaaaaaaaaaaaaaaalllllllllllll llllllllllllll!!!!!!!!!!!!!!!!!!!!

'Six games down, one to go!' Diego cheered at full-time. 'Come on, guys, we're so nearly there!'

In the World Cup final, Argentina faced West Germany in front of 115,000 fans. They knew it was going to be their toughest match yet, even when they went 2–0 up.

'Keep going!' Diego urged his teammates. 'West Germany *never* give up.'

He was right. With ten minutes to go, the score was 2–2.

'Uh-oh,' Diego thought to himself. For the first time all tournament, he was scared. Argentina couldn't lose in the final, not after taking the lead. This was their World Cup. They needed to dig deep and find a winner from somewhere.

That somewhere turned out to be Diego's lovely left boot. When his country needed him most, he saved the day yet again.

West Germany's Lothar Matthäus had been man-marking Diego all game and by the eighty-third minute, he wasn't the only one. But even with a crowd of players around him, Diego picked out the perfect pass to send 'Burru' through on goal. 3–2!

When the referee blew the final whistle, Diego went crazy. He ran around, hugging everybody.

'We did it! We did it!' he shouted over and over again.

Against the odds, Diego had achieved his childhood dream of leading Argentina to World Cup glory. He had made his nation proud again.

Campeones, Campeones, Olé! Olé! Olé!

Mar-a-Don-a! Mar-a-Don-a!

Vamos Vamos Argentina!

From start to finish, it had been Diego's tournament and he had the Best Player award to prove it. But the main prize was the World Cup trophy. With tears in his eyes, he raised it above his head and roared. He was a true national hero now.

CHAPTER 16

NAPOLI TITLE I

After a World Cup to remember, Diego didn't just kick back and relax. He had more trophies to win with Napoli. He returned to Italy, ready to conquer Serie A.

The club president, Corrado Ferlaino, had been busy building a title-winning team, with a little help from his star Number 10.

'What do we need to succeed?' he asked Diego.

'We need a clever centre-back like Alessandro Renica,' he replied.

Napoli signed Renica from Sampdoria.

'What else do we need?' Ferlaino asked.

'We need a good goalkeeper,' Diego said.

Napoli signed Claudio Garella from Verona.

'What else do we need?'

'We need strong strikers who can score.'

Napoli signed Bruno Giordano from Lazio and Andrea Carnevale from Udinese.

'Anything else?' Ferlaino asked.

Diego smiled. 'We need a little bit of luck, but I don't think you can buy that, President!'

Like Argentina at the 1986 World Cup, Napoli were the battling rebels, beating the big boys one by one. They were Diego's team, after all.

First up: Roma at the Stadio Olimpico. Bruno cut in from the left and chipped a great pass to Diego. With a touch of class, he controlled it perfectly and fired the ball into the bottom corner.

Goooooooooooooooooooooaaaaaaaaaaaaaaaaalllllllllllll llllllllllllll!!!!!!!!!!!!!!!!!!!!

1–0 to Napoli! Diego bounced up and down in front of the club's cheering fans. 'We can do this!'

Next up: the champions Juventus. It was first against second, the north of Italy against the south. Their rivalry was fierce, but Napoli hadn't won in

Turin for nearly thirty years.

'Forget about history,' Diego told his teammates before kick-off. 'All that matters is the next ninety minutes. Believe!'

Even when Juventus took the lead, Napoli never stopped believing. Captain Diego urged his team forward, looking for the equaliser. Moreno Ferrario finally got it with fifteen minutes to go, and their 20,000 fans roared with relief.

'Come on, there's plenty of time to score again!' Diego said with a smirk.

When Bruno made it 2–1, the fans started dancing in their seats. When Giuseppe Volpecina made it 3–1, they went absolutely wild.

Napoli! Napoli! Napoli!

The players and supporters all celebrated like they had just won the league. Unfortunately, they hadn't. There were still twenty-one massive matches to go, but Diego led his team past Empoli, past Udinese, past Torino...

Napoli! Napoli! Napoli!

However, by the time Juventus came to town,

looking for revenge, Napoli were still only three points clear at the top of the table. Roma and Inter Milan were snapping at their heels too.

'We have to win this,' Diego shouted passionately. 'We have to beat everybody!'

After fifteen minutes, Napoli won a free kick within shooting distance. Alessandro stood there next to Diego, but everyone assumed that the captain would strike it. They assumed wrong. Diego tapped it to Alessandro who took a stinging strike at goal. The ball slipped straight through the surprised keeper's hands and then through his legs too. 1–0!

The Stadio San Paolo sprang to life, with shouts and flags and hugs. Everyone now believed that it was going to be Napoli's season. They were finally going to become the Champions of Italy.

With four games to go, however, that dream was still in some doubt. If Napoli didn't beat AC Milan, Inter would overtake them.

'We can't let that happen!' their manager Ottavio Bianchi screamed at the top of his voice. 'We've been top all season and that's where we're going to finish!'

The Napoli players responded brilliantly. They had worked so hard to get this far. They weren't going to just throw it all away at the end.

Bruno crossed from the left and Andrea headed home. 1–0!

Bruno spotted Diego's run and played the perfect pass. Diego brought the ball down beautifully, dribbled round the keeper and scored from a difficult angle.

Goooooooooooooooooooooaaaaaaaaaaaaaaaaalllllllllllll llllllllllllllll!!!!!!!!!!!!!!!!!!!!!

He threw his arms up in the air with joy, as the fans chanted their hero's name:

Diego! Diego! Diego!

Napoli stayed top of Serie A, but they weren't safe yet. The tension was almost unbearable. They drew with Como... but Inter Milan lost to Ascoli!

'Today, we win the league,' Diego announced before the match against Fiorentina. It wasn't a possibility; it was a certainty.

With the home crowd cheering them on, Napoli's star strikeforce got the job done. Diego played a clever pass through to Andrea, who played a one-two with Bruno and shot past the keeper. 1–0!

In the end, Napoli didn't win the match but that didn't matter.

A cheer rang out around the stadium – Inter had lost to Atalanta!

A few seconds later, there was another cheer – Juventus had drawn with Verona!

By the time the final whistle blew, the good news had spread across the field. The title race was over, and Napoli were the Italian Champions for the first time ever. The party started right there on the pitch and it carried on all over Naples for days. It was the proudest achievement that the city and its people had ever known.

'We did it, we did it!' Ferlaino shouted, crying tears of joy.

'This is for all the people of Naples,' Diego told the TV cameras. 'This is for you!'

He would never forget their amazing welcome at the Stadio San Paolo three years earlier. The fans made Diego feel at home straight away. That day,

he promised to be their hero and he had kept that
promise. Now, his face was painted on murals all
over the city and new-born babies were named
'Diego' in his honour.

Napoli's season wasn't over quite yet, however.
They had the chance to become only the third Italian
team ever to win the League and Cup Double.

'Who did it before us?' Diego asked.

'Juventus and Torino.'

'Right, let's win it for the South then!'

Napoli beat Atalanta comfortably in the Coppa
Italia final to complete a sensational season. Diego
was having the time of his life. First, the 1986 World
Cup and now the Double with Napoli. Everything he
touched seemed to turn to gold.

CHAPTER 17

THE COPA AMÉRICA CHALLENGE

As Diego headed home for the summer, he was exhausted. His life felt like non-stop football. If he wasn't playing for his club, he was playing for his country. What he really needed was a rest, but there was no time for that. Diego was expected to lead Argentina to glory at the 1987 Copa América. As the hosts and world champions, they were the favourites to win the tournament.

'The whole nation is watching,' Bilardo reminded his players. 'Don't let them down!'

Diego was desperate to repeat their World Cup success, but unfortunately, he wasn't fully fit. His doctor had told him that his legs wouldn't recover properly unless they got two weeks of total rest.

'Two weeks!' he thought to himself. 'No way, the tournament starts *next* week!'

Diego missed the training sessions, but he couldn't miss the matches. His country was counting on him to be their hero.

He scored once against Peru, nutmegging the keeper.

He scored twice against Ecuador, a penalty and then a free kick.

'Vamos Argentina!' Diego shouted, swinging his fist above his head. Even after winning the World Cup, every goal still meant so much to him.

And every trophy too. This was Diego's third Copa América and only his first appearance in the semi-finals. Surely, a player with his talent had to win the tournament at least once in his career?

However, as he prepared for the game against Uruguay, Diego was ill as well as injured. His body was telling him to take a break.

'Are you sure you should be playing?' Tota asked him, sounding concerned. 'You've got a fever!'

'I have to, mamá,' he replied. 'I'm the captain, and you know I can't say no to my country!'

Although Diego played in the semi-final, he was a shadow of his usual self. He felt weak and sluggish, as if all his usual energy and passion had been drained from his body. Every time he tried to run, it felt like he was wading through water. None of his tricks worked and his shots flew wide. Perhaps, Diego had used up all of his luck in leading Napoli to the Double.

Uruguay took full advantage. They knocked Argentina out in front of their own fans.

'What an embarrassment!' the nation reacted angrily. 'What a disgrace!'

*

Two years later, in 1989, Diego was back to try again. With the next World Cup on the horizon, Argentina really needed to find their best form again.

'This is our last tournament before Italia 90,' Bilardo told his players. 'Let's give the fans something to get excited about!'

As time went by, Diego had become more and

more determined to add the Copa América to
his trophy collection. Argentina were the world
champions, so why weren't they also the South
American Champions?

'Come on, it's thirty years since we last won it,'
Diego reminded his teammates. 'I wasn't even born
then!'

Argentina got off to a good start, beating Chile
1–0. Diego passed back to Pedro Troglio, who fired
a fierce shot at goal. The keeper could only parry
it straight to Argentina's young forward, Claudio
Caniggia.

'Yes, Cani!' Diego cheered, lifting him up in the air.

Against Uruguay, Argentina played with ten men
for seventy-five minutes and still managed to win,
thanks to their solid defence and their new star
strikeforce.

As Diego turned with the ball in the busy midfield,
he spotted Claudio's run. With the outside of his left
boot, he lifted a perfect pass through to him. Claudio
shot first-time and beat the goalkeeper at his near
post.

'Yes, Diego!' he cheered, as his partner lifted him up into the air again.

There were positive signs for Argentina fans, but there were negative signs too. After a dull 0–0 draw against Ecuador, Bilardo was furious.

'You should all be ashamed!' he shouted in the dressing room. 'I expect to see effort and pride out there on the pitch. You're playing for your country!'

Unfortunately, a similar thing happened again against Bolivia. When teams sat deep and defended bravely, Argentina's attackers couldn't find a way through. Usually, it was Diego who saved the day with a moment of magic, but not this time. He tried and tried, but he ended up fouled and frustrated.

'Sorry, I'm not Superman,' Diego said in a post-match interview. 'I can't be the hero every time.'

Things got worse for Argentina as the tournament went on. Brazil beat them 2–0 and then so did Uruguay. In seven games, the team had only scored two goals. They had failed the Copa América challenge miserably yet again.

Argentina didn't seem to have a hope of winning

the World Cup again, but their captain wasn't giving up. He remembered hearing the same doom and gloom before the tournament in 1986.

'Cani, we can do this,' Diego declared confidently, 'but we've got a lot of work to do!'

CHAPTER 18

NAPOLI TITLE II

When Napoli won the Serie A title in 1987, Italian football fans described it as a miracle.

'It was a total fluke,' they decided. 'There's no way that they could do that again!'

Napoli didn't win the league in 1988 or 1989, but they didn't sink back to the bottom. They finished second in both seasons and in 1989, they won the UEFA Cup instead. Their leader Diego hadn't lost his golden touch at all. He destroyed every defence that he came up against.

In the semi-final against Bayern Munich, he set up both goals for Andrea Carnevale and new Brazilian strike partner, Careca.

In the final against Stuttgart, he scored a penalty

and set up more goals for Careca and Ciro Ferrara.

After more than sixty years, Napoli finally had their first ever European trophy. As Diego and his teammates celebrated on the pitch, the fans sang loudly and proudly for their heroes.

Napoli! Napoli! Napoli!

Diego! Diego! Diego!

So, what next? As the 1989–90 Serie A season began, everyone expected AC Milan to win the title. They had Franco Baresi, Roberto Donadoni, and the deadly Dutch trio – Ruud Gullit, Frank Rijkaard and Marco van Basten. They looked unbeatable.

'We'll see about that!' Diego said to himself.

At the Stadio San Paolo, Napoli thrashed AC Milan 3–0. Diego created the first two goals and scored the third himself. As he dribbled into the penalty area, he waited for the goalkeeper to dive and then coolly chipped the ball over him.

Goooooooooooooooooooooaaaaaaaaaaaaaaaaalllllllllllll lllllllllllllll!!!!!!!!!!!!!!!!!!!!

It was the kind of clever, cheeky finish that Diego used to love scoring on the *potreros* of Villa Fiorito.

Now, he had done it against one of the best football teams in the world.

'You genius!' Careca cheered.

The win sent out a clear message to the rest of the league: 'Don't write us off!'

Just in case anyone hadn't got the message, Napoli sent out another one when Inter Milan came to town. Careca got the first goal and Diego scored the second. From the edge of the area, he placed a perfect shot into the bottom corner.

Goooooooooooooooooooooaaaaaaaaaaaaaaaaalllllllllllll llllllllllllll!!!!!!!!!!!!!!!!!!!

As always, Diego charged off to celebrate in front of the supporters. 'Come on, we can do this!' he shouted.

Suddenly, the impossible seemed possible. With their captain on fire, the Napoli fans dared to dream of another league title. At Christmas, they still sat at the top of the table.

'We're not moving for anyone!' Diego declared.

In March, however, AC Milan beat Napoli at the San Siro and stole their number one spot away. Some players might have settled for second place, but not Diego.

'This isn't over yet!' he snarled.

Napoli had five massive matches to go, starting with their old rivals Juventus. In the tunnel, Diego walked all the way along the line, giving high-fives to each of his teammates. To win, they all had to work together.

These were the big games that Diego loved most, and he inspired Napoli to victory once again. Early on, the ball bounced to him in the Juventus penalty area. He knew that he wouldn't get a better chance. There were two defenders closing in but, with two quick touches, Diego turned and shot. The goalkeeper didn't even have time to move.

Goooooooooooooooooooooaaaaaaaaaaaaaaaaalllllllllllllll llllllllllllll!!!!!!!!!!!!!!!!!!!!!

Diego was on a roll and he had plenty more tricks up his sleeve. The Napoli fans cheered every single touch. He tormented the Juventus defence again and again with his pace and trickery. For a tiny playmaker, he had surprising strength and bravery. It was so difficult to stop him.

Diego battled on through tackle after tackle, until eventually three players fouled him at once. Free kick! He took one step, two step, and swung that lovely left foot. *Bang!* The ball curled up over the wall and then dipped down into the bottom corner.

Goooooooooooooooooooooaaaaaaaaaaaaaaaaalllllllllllll llllllllllllllll!!!!!!!!!!!!!!!!!!

That stunning strike nearly caused a riot in the Stadio San Paolo. Thanks to Diego's dazzling talent, their title dream was still alive!

Napoli! Napoli! Napoli!

With five minutes to go, the manager Alberto Bigon gave his captain a rest. As he walked off, Diego clapped the fans and they clapped him back until their hands got sore. What a hero! They loved him so much, like a member of their own family. Before Diego arrived, Napoli had nothing. Now, they had pride *and* glory.

'Four more wins, four more wins!' the players chanted together in the dressing room after the game. They knew that they could do it.

Napoli secured their first win against Atalanta, and

there was more good news to come. AC Milan could only draw against Bologna – they were tied at the top now, with forty-five points each.

Napoli secured their second win against Bari but this time, AC Milan won too.

'Don't worry, they're going to slip up again,' Diego predicted. 'But we're not going to, are we?'

'No!' his teammates boomed back.

As Napoli travelled to Bologna, some of their younger players were starting to feel the pressure. What if they let the fans down? Thankfully, Diego didn't know what nerves were. Failure didn't even cross his mind. He had enough confidence for the whole team and he shared it out generously.

'We can beat anyone, guys. ANYONE!'

'AC Milan, Inter Milan, Juventus – none of them thought we would get this far, but we did. None of them think we can win the league, but we will. WE WILL!'

As the match kicked off, they were all fired up and ready to win.

Giancarlo Corradini crossed to Careca, who

smashed the ball into the top corner. 1– 0!

Diego dribbled across the penalty area and curled the ball into the bottom corner. 2–0!

Careca backheeled it to Giovanni Francini, who steered the ball past the keeper. 3–0!

They were 3–0 up after fifteen minutes.

'Keep going guys!' Diego cheered. 'This is *our* season!'

Napoli secured their third win, but what about AC Milan? They lost 2–1 to Verona!

'One more win, one more win!' the Napoli players chanted together. They knew that they could do it.

Before the big game against Lazio, Naples prepared for its biggest party ever. The local people coloured the city blue and white, with balloons and banners everywhere.

'Look around you,' Bigon told his players. 'We have to win the league now!'

As the match kicked off, the atmosphere in the Stadio San Paolo was tense, but that didn't last long. Diego chipped a dangerous cross right onto Marco Baroni's head. 1–0!

After that, they just had to hold on. The second half felt like forever but eventually, the final whistle blew. It was official – Napoli were the Champions of Italy once more.

'Yesssss!' Diego shouted up at the sky.

His second Serie A title felt even better than the first. He had worked so hard for it, scoring so many important goals.

The fans clapped and cheered as he led his team on a lap of honour around the pitch.

Diego! Diego! Diego!

'Thank you, captain!' the Napoli president Corrado Ferlaino said, crying tears of joy once more.

The players, however, showed their appreciation in a different way. During a TV interview, they poured a bottle of champagne over Diego's head, singing:

Oh, mamá, mamá, mamá,
Do you know why
My heart beats fast?
I saw Maradona, I saw Maradona,
And, mamá, I fell in love!

CHAPTER 19

WORLD CUP 1990

As the 1990 World Cup kicked off, Diego was feeling better than ever. At the age of twenty-nine, he was hitting his footballing peak. His fitness was great and so was his form. He had always had the talent but now he had the experience to go with it.

After winning his second Serie A title, Diego was hungry for more glory. A second World Cup trophy was top of his wish list. Could Argentina go all the way again? The hopes of the nation rested on the broad shoulders of their captain and star Number 10.

'We will only do well if Maradona plays well,' the people argued.

'He's our only hope!' they declared.

It was a good thing that Diego was used to playing under pressure. Napoli depended on him and so did Argentina. He wasn't going to let them down, and he wasn't going to let go of the World Cup trophy without a real fight.

'Everyone expects us to fail,' he told his teammates, 'so let's prove them wrong!'

Proving people wrong was his favourite thing to do. Italy were the tournament hosts and Argentina would play their second and third matches at the Stadio San Paolo, Diego's home.

'It's a sign!' he thought to himself excitedly.

Before that, however, Argentina got off to a shocking start. Against Cameroon, Diego was man-handled and man-marked out of the game. Benjamin Massing followed him everywhere, ready to stop him at all costs.

'I need some help here!' Diego called out in frustration.

So, who else could step up and be Argentina's hero? Abel Balbo shot wide, then Jorge Burruchaga, then Oscar Ruggeri. Their fans grew more and more restless but when Cameroon's André Kana-Biyik was sent off in the second half, they breathed a sigh of relief. With an extra player, surely they would now go on and win.

Vamos Vamos Argentina!

But it was Cameroon who scored instead to leave Argentina in despair. Diego couldn't believe it.

'Come on, this is a World Cup!' he screamed out to get his team going. 'And we're the world champions!'

They certainly weren't playing like world champions. For the last few minutes, it was Argentina's eleven men against Cameroon's nine, and still they couldn't score. At the final whistle, they were booed off the pitch.

Argentina had a choice to make: 'Either we go home now, or we come back fighting!' Diego told his disappointed teammates in the dressing room.

As their captain hoped, they chose to come back fighting. At the Stadio San Paolo, Argentina beat the Soviet Union and drew with Romania. It wasn't the homecoming that Diego had been hoping for, but he was playing through pain. His left knee, his left ankle, the big toe on his right foot – everything was hurting.

'Can you carry on?' Bilardo asked him.

Diego glared back. 'Of course, I can!'

In the second round, Argentina faced Brazil in Turin. It didn't get much tougher than that. On the pitch, Diego would be up against his Napoli teammates, Careca and Alemão. And in the stands, he would be booed by thousands of Juventus fans.

Diego couldn't wait. 'I love being the villain!' he joked with Cani.

For eighty minutes, Brazil attacked, and Argentina defended.

'Hang in there!' Diego urged his tired teammates. He needed to find a moment of magic from somewhere…

He got the ball just inside his own half. With a clever change of direction, he burst through the Brazil midfield and dribbled towards their defence. Even with injuries, he was still the quickest on the counter-attack. The fans jumped to their feet with great belief. How many times had their hero saved them like this?

Vamos Vamos Argentina!

As Diego ran to the right, Cani ran to the left. The plan worked perfectly. Brazil's defenders all rushed towards the danger man and forgot about Argentina's other attacker. Diego hadn't, though. When the time was right, he slipped the ball through to Cani, who dribbled past the goalkeeper and scored. 1–0!

'Come on!' Diego roared with a mix of joy and relief. What a goal, what a victory.

Cameroon had shocked Argentina, but now Argentina had shocked Brazil. With that win, they sent out a clear message to the football world: 'Don't write us off!'

At last, Argentina had rediscovered their winning spirit. They weren't pretty to watch, but they were getting the job done. First, they battled past Yugoslavia in the quarter-finals and then past the hosts Italy in the semi-finals. Both matches went to penalties, and both times, they held their nerve to win.

Diego's spot-kick against Yugoslavia was saved but

he made no mistake against Italy. He calmly stepped up and sent Walter Zenga the wrong way. The fans cheered and so did Diego as he jumped into his teammates' arms.

He wasn't Argentina's hero that time, however. Sergio Goycochea, their incredible goalkeeper, saved two penalties to send his country into another World Cup final.

'Yes, yes, YES!' Diego screamed at the centre of the big team hug.

It was an amazing achievement, especially after their slow start to the tournament. As he left the pitch, he waved to the fans and kissed the Argentina badge on his shirt. Competing for his country meant everything to him.

The final was a repeat of 1986 – Argentina vs West Germany. Could they win it again? Diego believed in his teammates. Argentina no longer had the same skill in their squad, but they had the same strength and spirit.

'That beautiful trophy is *ours*,' Diego declared, 'and it's not going anywhere!'

Argentina stuck to their game plan and defended brilliantly. In the eighty-fifth minute, however, all that hard work went to waste. Rudi Völler fell to the floor after a tackle from Roberto Sensini, and the referee gave a penalty.

'No way, he got the ball!' the Argentina players protested angrily.

But Andreas Brehme scored from the spot and crushed Diego's dream of winning back-to-back World Cups.

'We've been robbed!' he groaned.

It was a cruel, cruel blow for his beloved Argentina. They had come so close to glory again. At the final whistle, Diego cried and cried. He couldn't bear to carry on.

'I love being the captain of my country,' he announced, 'but this is the end. I'm leaving.'

CHAPTER 20

FALSE START AT SEVILLA

After the World Cup, Diego's dark days continued. He returned to Napoli, but things weren't the same anymore. His passion for football had disappeared and he began getting in trouble off the pitch and neglecting his training. Time and time again, the Napoli fans forgave their hero, even though he was doing more harm than good.

'We have to stand by him,' they agreed. 'Where would this club be without Maradona?'

Eventually, however, enough was enough. When Diego was suspended from football for fifteen months for bad behaviour, the Napoli fans gave up on him. They felt so betrayed.

'We've given him so much love and what does he do with it? Throw it back in our faces!'

Diego's incredible career in Italy was over. He would miss Naples so much, and he was sorry for letting the wonderful people down. It was time, however, to move on. He returned to Argentina and thought long and hard about his future in football.

Did Diego still want to play the beautiful game? Yes, but where?

Was it time to return to Boca Juniors? That was his dream, but they didn't have enough money to buy him. Besides, Diego wasn't yet ready to leave Europe behind. He still had a point to prove once his suspension was over.

'Who wants me?' Diego asked his agent. 'I'll go anywhere!'

What about Marseille? After the stresses of Italy, France would be nice and peaceful...

Or Sevilla? They were a good team and Diego's old Argentina manager, Carlos Bilardo, was now in charge.

'Come join me, you'll love it here!' Bilardo told

him. 'It's the perfect place for you. We've got a strong squad and you can play without all that crazy pressure.'

That did sound perfect. Diego travelled to Sevilla to meet with their president, Luis Cuervas.

'This is the club for you,' he argued passionately. 'We're crying out for a new superstar to lead us to glory!'

Diego certainly fitted the bill. He stayed to watch the team's next game at the Ramón Sánchez Pizjuán Stadium. Although Sevilla lost to Deportivo la Coruña, he really enjoyed the experience. The goosebumps were back as he cheered on the team's talented players like Diego 'Cholo' Simeone and Davor Šuker. It already felt like home, like another Napoli. The fans greeted him like a hero.

'Sign for us, Diego!' they begged. 'We need you!'

And so he did. The deal took time but at last, the exciting news spread: 'Sevilla have just signed the best player in the world!'

Eight years after leaving Barcelona, Diego was back in Spanish football. He couldn't wait to get back to doing what he did best – entertaining the world with his lovely left foot and silky skills. His kit colour had changed from Napoli's blue to Sevilla's white and red, but Diego was still the Number 10 and he was still the captain.

'We are going to be champions!' he told journalists with a big smile on his face.

Some people, of course, had their doubts about Diego. He hadn't played professional football for a long time and he looked unfit. And what about that golden touch – did he still have it?

Yes! On his debut against his old enemies Athletic Bilbao, Diego set up Sevilla's goal with a trademark free kick. A week later, he scored the winner against Real Zaragoza.

'Come on, let's win the league!' Diego screamed as the adrenaline rushed through his body. The old buzz was back, and he felt like he could achieve anything again.

He worked hard to get fitter and stronger. He meant business. He even had his hair cut to look like the Diego of 1986, that amazing year when he led

Argentina to World Cup glory.

On the pitch, Diego scored a free kick against Celta Vigo and a volley against Sporting Gijon. He saved his most magical masterclass, however, for when Real Madrid visited town. Diego had destroyed them with Barcelona and he destroyed them once again with Sevilla. It was one of his best performances of all time and the fans cheered every flick and every trick.

Diego! Diego! Diego!

He was so glad to be back to his flying best, living up to the expectations of a legend. Sevilla moved up to sixth place in La Liga.

Sadly, however, Diego's Spanish success didn't last long. Argentina's new manager Coco Basile had been keeping a close eye on Diego's return to form. He wanted him to come back and play for the national team again.

'You've got a big part to play at the 1994 World Cup,' the manager told him.

That was music to Diego's ears. When it came to his beloved Argentina, he couldn't say no.

After three years out, he was ready for his big international comeback. He had missed his role as national hero.

'I'm in!' Diego told Basile. Unfortunately, however, a fight soon broke out between club and country.

'He is going to play for us against Brazil and Denmark,' Argentina ordered.

Basile shook his head. 'No, he can play against Brazil, but not against Denmark. It's a long journey and we need to keep him fit and healthy.'

Argentina agreed to that deal, but Diego didn't. His country was now his priority and so he played both matches anyway. By the time he returned to Spain, he was exhausted, and Sevilla lost 2–0 to Logroñés.

Diego was in big trouble. He had disobeyed his club, and everyone was furious with him – his teammates, the fans, the president and the manager.

'You were doing so well!' Bilardo shouted at his superstar. 'Why did you have to go and ruin it?'

But Diego had made his decision – his country came first, now and forever. He stayed in Spain until the end of the season and then returned to Argentina.

What next? The 1994 World Cup was still a whole year away. At Sevilla, Diego had shown fantastic flashes of his old genius. There was still magic in his feet and so, back in his home country, he signed for Newell's Old Boys.

'I have to keep playing if I want to make Basile's squad,' he told his old Argentina teammate Ricardo Giusti.

People said that one last World Cup was impossible, but when it came to Diego, anything was always possible.

CHAPTER 21

WORLD CUP 1994

Diego didn't make Basile's squad for Argentina's match against Colombia. Instead, he sat in the stands of the Monumental Stadium with his dad, cheering on his country.

Vamos Vamos Argentina!

Oscar Ruggeri was now the captain in defence, with Fernando Redondo and Diego's old Sevilla teammate 'Cholo' Simeone in midfield, and new superstar Gabriel Batistuta in attack. It looked like a solid line-up but where was the skilful Number 10? They were missing that Maradona magic.

After fifty minutes, Argentina were losing 2–0. After eighty-five minutes, they were losing 5–0. 5–0!

Diego couldn't believe what he was watching. What a disaster! It was one of the national team's worst-ever defeats and they were now in danger of missing out on the 1994 World Cup in the USA.

The fans looked away in disgust and began calling for their hero:

'Come back, Diego, come back!'

Tears filled his eyes as he listened to his name being chanted. Diego was ready to rescue Argentina. He began working even harder with his personal trainer, Daniel Cerroni. One training session a day became two training sessions a day, and sometimes even three! Diego was determined once more. At thirty-three, this was his last opportunity and he didn't want to waste it.

To make it to the World Cup, Argentina would have to beat Australia. Basile brought Diego back into the team for the big games and gave him the captain's armband.

'Lead us to victory!' his manager told him.

Gabriel held the ball up well and then passed to Diego on the right. With a quick flick of the left boot,

he was off! He raced past the first defender and cut
inside past the second.

Olé!

Eventually, Diego was tackled but he didn't give
up. He jumped up and chased after the ball until he
won it back.

'Diego! Diego! Diego!' the fans cheered. They
loved his fighting spirit.

Diego shifted the ball onto his left foot and curled
a brilliant cross into the box. Abel Balbo was there to
head home. 1–0 to Argentina!

Abel ran towards Diego, pointing and smiling. 'It's
great to have you back!' he shouted.

It was great to *be* back, and to hear the fans going
wild in the stadium. When his nation needed him
most, Diego never let them down.

Argentina were through to the World Cup, and
he couldn't wait. As long as he stayed fit, Diego
would get to play in his fourth tournament. That
thought kept him going during the tough months
of training.

'How are you feeling?' Basile asked him.

'I feel like a plane,' Diego replied. 'I feel like I could fly!'

As the squad landed in America, Diego was full of enthusiasm and full of hope. He couldn't help it – it was the World Cup, his favourite event! He felt like an excited teenager again, about to play for the first time.

'We can win this!' Diego told his teammates.

In 1990, Argentina had started the World Cup slowly, like a chugging old car. In 1994, however, they raced to top speed, like a brand-new Ferrari. With Diego, Gabriel, Abel and Cani all attacking together, Greece had no chance. They were 1–0 down after only two minutes, and Argentina were just getting going.

Gabriel flicked the ball to Diego, who flicked it through to Cholo.

Olé! Olé!

The fans were enjoying the entertainment. Cholo crossed to the back post but Cani couldn't quite reach it.

'Unlucky, keep going!' Diego clapped and cheered. This was football at its finest.

Even their defenders got involved. José Chamot dribbled forward and passed to Gabriel. *Bang*! 2–0!

In the second half, Argentina gave Greece a painful lesson in quick, one-touch passing. On the edge of the penalty area, they moved the ball from Fernando to Diego, back to Fernando, to Cani, back to Fernando, to Diego.

Olé! Olé! Olé! Olé! Olé!

It was time to score. Diego created a bit of space for himself and curled the ball into the top corner.

Goooooooooooooooooooooaaaaaaaaaaaaaaaaalllllllllllll llllllllllllll!!!!!!!!!!!!!!!!!!

What a moment! Diego raced towards the fans, roaring and nodding his head as if to say, 'Yes, I've still got it. I'm still a genius!'

With that 4–0 win, Argentina became the World Cup team to watch.

Even in their next game, when Nigeria took the lead, they never stopped believing. With so many amazing attackers, surely someone would save the day for Argentina. Cani got the goals but they were both thanks to Diego's clever free kicks.

For the first goal, Diego pretended to shoot but back-heeled the ball to Gabriel instead. Gabriel fired off a fierce long-range shot, so fierce that the goalkeeper couldn't hold it. Cani pounced on the rebound. 1–1!

'Come on!' Diego shouted, jumping into his teammate's arms.

For the second goal, Diego was about to chip the ball into the box, when he heard Cani calling his name on the left wing.

'Diego, Diego I'm free! Play it now!'

He took it quickly and Cani dribbled through and scored. 2–1!

Argentina looked unstoppable, and so did Captain Diego. But as he prepared for their next match against Bulgaria, he received some very bad news. He had failed a medical test.

'That weight loss medicine you've been taking – they think you've been getting an unfair advantage from it. They say you've cheated,' Basile told him.

'No, that's not possible!' Diego argued, fighting back the tears. 'We checked with FIFA's doctors – it was OK.'

He couldn't leave the World Cup – not now and not like this. He hadn't done anything wrong. Diego's return to form was due to hard work, not cheating.

'Daniel, what's going on?' he cried out. 'Help!'

His personal trainer looked down at the floor. 'I'm so sorry, I made a mistake. I gave you the wrong medicine.'

Diego's World Cup was over. He watched the start of the Bulgaria game on TV in his hotel room but after a while, he had to turn it off. It was heartbreaking to see his talented teammates struggling without him. They were missing that Maradona magic.

After Argentina lost 2–0, Fernando told Diego, 'Every time I got the ball, I was looking for you out there.'

A few days later, Argentina were knocked out by Romania. After that stunning start, their World Cup dream had been destroyed.

Diego was devastated. 'I wanted to end my international career with pride, not shame,' he cried.

CHAPTER 22

BACK TO BOCA

Diego was suspended from football for another fifteen months. Was this the end of the road for him? His international career was over, but what about his club career? His legs and ankles were telling him to stop but his head and heart disagreed.

'We want more!' they cried out.

In 1995, Diego won the Ballon d'Or award for his incredible career. It was a very proud and emotional moment as he held the heavy, glittering trophy in his hands.

'Thank you, it's a great honour,' Diego said, but with a sad smile because he wasn't ready to say goodbye yet. He wanted one last football adventure.

Pelé called and asked him to become the player-manager of his club Santos in Brazil.

'Thanks, but no thanks,' Diego replied. There was only one club that he wanted to play for. His dream was to go back to Boca Juniors.

With a little help from his friends, that dream came true. By the time his ban ended, Diego was back at the Bombonera and back in the blue and gold Number 10 shirt. After thirteen years, he was home again.

'Let's do this!' he shouted to Cani. Argentina's amazing attackers were together again.

Diego celebrated his return by dying a golden streak through his hair. He waved and clapped as the fans cheered his name.

Diego! Diego! Diego!

What a welcome home party! Confetti, balloons and streamers filled the air and scattered across the grass. The confetti was still there when the match kicked off.

Diego's second match for Boca was even more special. He was up against his first club, Argentinos Juniors, and his own nephew, Dany.

'Good luck!' they said to each other before kick-off.

In the first half, Dany managed to keep his uncle quiet, but Diego was determined to win. In the seventieth minute, Boca won a free kick just outside the penalty area. One step, two step, *bang*! He whipped the ball over the Argentinos wall and into the top corner.

Gooooooooooooooooooooaaaaaaaaaaaaaaaaaallllllllllll llllllllllllll!!!!!!!!!!!!!!!!!!!!!

At first, Diego wasn't sure whether he should celebrate or not. He didn't want to disrespect his old team, and so he didn't jump around screaming like normal. At the same time, however, it was his comeback goal for Boca. After jogging back to the halfway line, Diego hugged his teammates and fell to his knees.

'Yes!' he shouted up at the sky. It felt so good to be the hero again.

Diego! Diego! Diego!

What about one last trophy? Diego had won the league with Boca in 1981, but could they do it again?

If so, they would make it to the Copa Libertadores, South America's biggest club competition.

'And we could win that too!' he thought to himself.

Diego did his best to lead Boca to victory, but in the end, they finished second behind Vélez Sarsfield.

'I'm sorry, we got so close!' he told the fans.

'Don't worry, we still love you!' they replied.

By 1996, Diego's health was getting worse. Boca started saving him for the biggest games, like the *Superclásico* against rivals River Plate.

With the Bombonera crowd behind him, Diego slipped the ball through to Cani, who crossed to José Basualdo. 1–0!

In the second half, Diego had the chance to make it 4–0 from the penalty spot. He coolly sent the goalkeeper the wrong way, but the ball bounced back off the post! Thankfully, Cani was there to complete his hat-trick.

'4–1! 4–1!' they cheered together at the final whistle, as fireworks fizzed across the sky.

A year later, in 1997, Diego chose the *Superclásico*

for his farewell to football. In the tunnel, he gathered his teammates around him.

'This is it for me. I want to go out with a win, okay?'

'Yes!' they all cheered together.

As Diego walked out onto the pitch for the last time, he threw his arms up like a champion.

'We'll miss you, Diego!' the fans shouted.

He was going to miss them too. It would be great to say goodbye with a goal. The ball came towards him on the left side of the penalty area. Diego watched it carefully and struck it sweetly on the volley. For a moment, it looked like his shot was heading for the bottom corner, but the goalkeeper made a good save.

'No, what was that?' Diego scolded himself. 'You can do better than that!'

The crowd let out a groan of disappointment. Their hero deserved a grand finale, but sadly, it wasn't to be. Boca won the match 2–1 but by then, Diego had already left the field to a standing ovation.

'Goodbye!' he cried, blowing kisses at the crowd.

Football would never forget Diego – his passion and

his genius, his 'Hand of God' and his 'Goal of the Century'.

Tota and Chitoro's little boy had been born to be a star. His magical feet had danced all the way from the dirt tracks of Villa Fiorito to three World Cup finals. He was the greatest Number 10 that the world had ever seen, a hero to millions of fans everywhere.

Diego was also born to be a leader. Despite all the injuries and personal problems, he never gave up and neither did the teams he captained. With style and skill, goals and guts, he took Napoli from nowhere to win two Italian League titles and a UEFA Cup trophy. He gave the people pride and joy.

But for Diego, his country always came first. No achievement could ever compare to his leading his beloved Argentina to World Cup glory in 1986. When his nation needed him most, Diego didn't let them down.

THE NEXT MARADONA

For the next ten years, Argentina searched for
'The Next Maradona', a superstar who could lead
the national team to World Cup glory again. They
reached the quarter-finals in 1998 but then crashed
out in the group stage in 2002.

'We need a new hero!' the fans cried out.

Every tiny, talented playmaker that came along
was described as 'The Next Maradona' – Ariel
Ortega, Juan Román Riquelme, Pablo Aimar, Andrés
D'Alessandro. They were all good, but not *that* good.
Being compared to a legend was an awful lot to live
up to.

'Perhaps we'll never have another player like

Diego,' they started to think.

But just when Argentina were giving up their search, along came a new wonderkid from Rosario.

Was he small? Yes!

Was he skilful? Yes!

Was he left-footed? Yes!

Could he score goals? Yes!

Even Diego was impressed. 'I have seen the player who will take my place in Argentinian football, and his name is Lionel Messi. Messi is a genius.'

Lionel, however, didn't want to be 'The Next Maradona'.

'Diego is Diego, and for me he is the greatest player of all time. I want to make my own World Cup history.'

Turn the page for a sneak preview of another brilliant football story by Matt and Tom Oldfield. . .

LIONEL MESSI

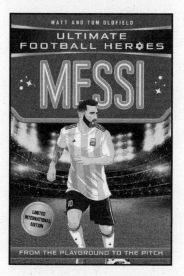

Available now!

CHAPTER 1

TREBLE TIME

'Hey, how's it going?' Lionel said, giving his fellow Argentinian Carlos Tevez a big hug as they waited in the tunnel.

Lionel was about to play in the 2014–15 Champions League final but he wasn't nervous at all. It was the third time he had played in the final with Barcelona and he had won both times before. He was a born winner and he was the best player in the world. So he felt very confident as he walked out on to the pitch at the Olympiastadion in Berlin to face Italian giants Juventus.

Lionel looked up into the stands and saw the huge wall of red and blue, or '*azulgrana*' as they called it in Spanish – the colours representing Barcelona, one of the world's biggest clubs and Lionel's home since the age of thirteen. He had played in some amazing Barcelona teams but this was perhaps the best team of all. They had already won the Spanish League and the Spanish Cup – now could they win the Champions League to make it an incredible Treble?

'Yes we can!' they cheered together.

Lionel's old friends Gerard Piqué and Javier Mascherano were the rocks in defence, Andrés Iniesta and Xavi controlled the midfield, while 'MSN' scored the goals up front. That's what the media were calling the world's best ever strikeforce – Lionel Messi, the Uruguayan Luis Suárez, and the Brazilian Neymar. Together, they had scored 120 goals already, with one big game left to play.

'Come on!' Lionel shouted as they waited for kick-off. When he was younger, he was too shy to speak to his teammates but he was twenty-seven now and one of their leaders.

Within four minutes, Neymar passed to Andrés, who passed to Ivan Rakitić, who scored. Barcelona

were 1-0 up. They made everything look so easy
with their quick, passing football, and Lionel hadn't
even been involved – but he knew how important
teamwork was.

'Great work!' he shouted to Ivan. Even he couldn't
do everything on his own.

Playing just behind Neymar and Luis, Lionel kept
searching for the space to work his magic. He was
known as The Flea, buzzing around everywhere and
terrorising his opponents. With his close control,
quick feet and footballing brain, he only ever needed
one second. Especially in his favourite area: just
outside the penalty area on the right side, he could
dribble with his amazing left foot. Lionel loved
scoring goals but he loved creating goals too – there
was nothing he couldn't do.

Barcelona were playing well but in the second
half, Juventus equalised. Just when his team needed
him most, Lionel came alive. He passed to Neymar,
who flicked it back to Lionel, who passed to Luis,
who passed back to Lionel. His shot went wide but
'MSN' were looking dangerous.

'If we keep this up, we'll score again!' Lionel told the others.

Minutes later, he dribbled forward again. The defender tried to tackle him but Lionel was too quick and too skilful. When he grabbed his shirt, Lionel shrugged him off. He wasn't the biggest footballer but he had worked hard to build up his strength.

As Lionel flew towards goal, Neymar made a run to make space for him. On the edge of the penalty area, Lionel decided to shoot. The ball flew straight at the goalkeeper but it swerved and dipped and he couldn't hold on to it. Luis sprinted towards the ball and smashed it into the net. 2-1!

As Luis jumped the advertising board, Lionel and Neymar were right behind him. It was yet another 'MSN' goal and Barcelona were one step closer to another Champions League trophy.

'There's plenty of time to score another!' Neymar said with a big smile on his face. Their favourite form of defence was attack.

In injury time, a clearance fell to Lionel. He looked up and saw his Brazilian teammate sprinting forward.

Stretching out his leg, he played a perfect through-ball. Neymar and Luis had a two-on-one against the Juventus centre-back. Neymar passed to Luis and as the defender moved across, Luis passed it back to Neymar. His shot rocketed into the bottom corner. 3-1! Barcelona were the Champions of Europe.

At the final whistle, Lionel hugged Andrés and Xavi. Together, they had conquered the football world again. He was so grateful to his amazing teammates. Their clever passes always arrived at his feet, no matter where he was on the pitch.

'After my injuries last year, some people thought that my best days were over,' Lionel said. 'They were so wrong!'

In the 2014/15 season he had helped Barcelona win the Treble with 58 goals and 25 assists in only 57 games. He was very proud of his return to form.

As Xavi lifted the trophy into the air, Lionel was right at the centre of the celebrations. He hadn't scored a goal in the final this time round, but he had still played a very important role.

'Thiago!' Lionel called to his three-year-old son,

who was wearing a Barcelona shirt with '10 MESSI' on the back. He kissed his girlfriend Antonella and carried Thiago around the pitch to wave to the fans. His little family meant the world to him.

'Look, there's your Grandpa and Grandma!' Lionel said to Thiago, pointing to Jorge and Celia in the crowd.

Without the love and support of his parents, Lionel wouldn't have made the brave move from Argentina to Spain to chase his dream of playing professional football. He had arrived at Barcelona as a tiny teenager with amazing natural talent but some of his coaches had their doubts. Did he really have the strength and desire to make it to the very top?

Nearly fifteen years later, the answer was there in Lionel's trophy cabinet: seven La Liga titles, four Champions League trophies, four FIFA Ballon d'Or trophies and one Olympic Gold Medal. He was the best player in the world but The Flea had plenty more magic up his sleeve.

DIEGO MARADONA HONOURS

Boca Juniors
🏆 Argentina Metropolitano League: 1981

Barcelona
🏆 Copa del Rey: 1983
🏆 Copa de la Liga: 1983

Napoli
🏆 Serie A: 1986–87, 1989–90
🏆 Coppa Italia: 1986–87
🏆 UEFA Cup: 1988–89

Argentina

🏆 FIFA U-20 World Cup: 1979

🏆 FIFA World Cup: 1986

Individual

🏆 FIFA U-20 World Cup Golden Ball: 1979

🏆 Argentine Football Writers' Footballer of the Year: 1979, 1980, 1981, 1986

🏆 South American Footballer of the Year: 1979, 1980

🏆 FIFA World Cup Golden Ball: 1986

🏆 FIFA World Cup Most Assists: 1986

🏆 FIFA World Cup All-Star Team: 1986, 1990

🏆 Serie A top scorer: 1987–88

🏆 Coppa Italia top scorer: 1987–88

🏆 South American Team of the Year: 1995

🏆 Ballon d'Or: 1996

🏆 World Team of the 20th Century: 1998

🏆 FIFA Player of the Century: 2000

🏆 FIFA Goal of the Century: 2002

MARADONA

THE FACTS

10

NAME: Diego Armando Maradona Franco

DATE OF BIRTH: 30 October 1960

AGE: 57

PLACE OF BIRTH: Buenos Aires

NATIONALITY: Argentinian

BEST FRIEND: Claudio Caniggia

MAIN CLUB: Boca Juniors, Barcelona and Napoli

POSITION: RW

THE STATS

Height (cm):	165
Club appearances:	590
Club goals:	312
Club trophies:	9
International appearances:	91
International goals:	34
International trophies:	1
Ballon d'Ors:	1

★ ★ ★ **HERO RATING: 95** ★ ★ ★

GREATEST MOMENTS

Type and search the web links to see the magic for yourself!

⭐ **1**

7 SEPTEMBER 1979, ARGENTINA 3-1 SOVIET UNION

https://www.youtube.com/watch?v=0A87S8gOjow&t=13s
Diego missed out on the Argentina squad for the 1978 World Cup, but he really made up for lost game-time at the Under-20 World Cup a year later. In Japan, Diego led his country all the way to the final, where he secured victory in style with a brilliant free-kick. He won the tournament's Best Player award and never looked back.

⭐2 26 JUNE 1983, REAL MADRID 2-2 BARCELONA

https://www.youtube.com/watch?v=OlAtlSa0Ol0&t=101s

Diego was always a big-game player. When he moved to Barcelona, his best performances came in El Clásico, the huge derby against Real Madrid. In 1983, Diego inspired his team to two cup final victories over their rivals. When he scored this wondergoal, even the Real Madrid fans clapped him.

⭐3 22 JUNE 1986, ARGENTINA 2-1 ENGLAND

https://www.youtube.com/watch?v=tMn7l3rlmWk

The 1986 World Cup was Diego's World Cup. He led Argentina to glory with skill, style and spirit. No game showed his genius more than the quarter-final against England. Minutes after scoring with 'The Hand of God', Diego dribbled from his own half, past five defenders, and scored 'the Goal of the Century'.

⭐ 4   25 MARCH 1990, NAPOLI 3-1 JUVENTUS

https://www.youtube.com/watch?v=FAuBHKtAbvM&t=141s

In four amazing years, Diego took Napoli from nowhere to two league titles. The first in 1987 was special but the second in 1990 was even better. Under pressure from AC Milan, Napoli held their nerve. In this crucial clash against rivals Juventus, Diego stole the show with two goals, including another excellent free-kick.

⭐ 5   21 JUNE 1994, ARGENTINA 4-0 GREECE

https://www.youtube.com/watch?v=aFToKtg3DTE

No-one expected Diego to make it to the 1994 World Cup in the USA, but as always, he proved people wrong. Not only did he make it, but he was one of Argentina's stars. Against Greece, Diego finished off a great team move by curling the ball into the top corner. Scoring for his country meant so much to him, although the tournament ended in disaster.

PLAY LIKE YOUR HEROES

THE DIEGO MARADONA 'GOAL OF THE CENTURY'

SEE IT HERE **You** Tube

https://www.youtube.com/watch?v=1wVho3I0NtU

STEP 1: Drop deep into your own half.

STEP 2: Keep an eye out for defenders and keep the ball under close control.

STEP 3: Use your quick feet to turn and face the goal, and then go! Burst forward as fast as you can, with the ball glued to your foot.

STEP 4: When a defender rushes towards you, change direction at the last second to fool them.

STEP 5: Be ready to jump! As you weave towards goal, you may face some fierce, flying tackles. Don't let them stop you.

STEP 6: Remember, you want this to be the ultimate wondergoal, so don't shoot until you have to. Instead, take the ball round the goalkeeper before walking it into the net.

TEST YOUR KNOWLEDGE

QUESTIONS

1. How old was Diego when he received his first football?

2. What was the name of Red Star's biggest rivals on the *potreros* in Villa Fiorito?

3. What was the name of Diego's friend who got him a trial at 'Little Onions'?

4. How old was Diego when he made his Argentinos Juniors debut?

5. Which Italian defender marked Diego out of the game at the 1982 World Cup?

6. Who did Diego replace as Argentina captain?

7. How many times did Diego destroy Real Madrid in his first season at Barcelona?

8. How many times did Diego win the Copa América with Argentina?

9. Which team did Diego's Napoli beat to the Serie A title in 1990?

10. How many World Cups did Diego play in for Argentina?

11. Diego won the Ballon d'Or – true or false?

Answers below. . . No cheating!

1. *Three years old* 2. *Tres Banderas, or 'Three Flags'* 3. Gregorio 'Goyo' Carrizo 4. *15 years old* 5. Claudio Gentile 6. Daniel Passarella 7. *Five* 8. Zero 9. AC Milan 10. *4 – 1982, 1986, 1990 and 1994* 11. *True – but only in 1996, at the end of his career.*

The 2018 World Cup saw your favourite football heroes go head-to head for the ultimate prize – the World Cup.

Complete your collection with six limited-edition international Ultimate Football Heroes.

AVAILABLE NOW

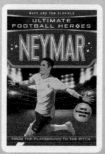

FOLLOW IN THE FOOTSTEPS OF LEGENDS. . .

Bridge the gap between past and present by stepping into the shoes of six classic World Cup heroes and reading their exciting stories – from the playground to the pitch, and to superstardom!

AVAILABLE NOW

MATT AND TOM OLDFIELD
CLASSIC FOOTBALL HEROES
BECKHAM
FROM THE PLAYGROUND TO THE PITCH

MATT AND TOM OLDFIELD
CLASSIC FOOTBALL HEROES
ZIDANE
FROM THE PLAYGROUND TO THE PITCH

MATT AND TOM OLDFIELD
CLASSIC FOOTBALL HEROES
KLINSMANN
FROM THE PLAYGROUND TO THE PITCH

MATT AND TOM OLDFIELD
CLASSIC FOOTBALL HEROES
MARADONA
FROM THE PLAYGROUND TO THE PITCH

MATT AND TOM OLDFIELD
CLASSIC FOOTBALL HEROES
FIGO
FROM THE PLAYGROUND TO THE PITCH

MATT AND TOM OLDFIELD
CLASSIC FOOTBALL HEROES
RONALDO
FROM THE PLAYGROUND TO THE PITCH